A Mother's Intuition: Autism – A Journey into Forgiveness & Healing

Written by: Catherine Marinelli – Gagliano

As told by: Linda Pedreira

Armando Marinelli
September 24, 1936 - September 19, 2021

Table of Contents

"A Mother's Intuition"
Foreword ("Forward")

The book goes from the present to the past; it is written in a non-chronological order to give readers an idea of how my life proceeds. What I mean is that, although the life of a parent of a child with special needs may appear to be topsy-turvy to those on the outside, there is a definite plan going on. Sometimes we take one step forward and three steps back, but the progress is there. It's just not measured in a typical fashion and that is why the book's format is an atypical one.

Volume I

Chapter 1
"GO CHIEFS"
The Element of Surprise

In the summer of 2013, my son Michael was going through a definite transformation. I guess you could say that he was really coming into himself. He appeared to always be in deep thought, thinking about the excitement of going to a new middle school, making new friends, and leaving elementary school and his painful past behind. He would openly discuss bullying and question why it was so difficult for children and adults to just accept the differences that exist in everyone. There was a time in the recent past when I couldn't have had these discussions with him because it would have hurt us so badly. He was being tormented to such a point that he was experiencing night terrors, anxiety and a true loathing of school.

Wow! How time flies. Michael was now entering into middle school and looking forward to playing football. He had taken a break from the sport due to the incessant teasing and harassment. (Michael had been diagnosed with ADHD, which did not truly explain his panic attacks both on and off the playing field.) When he attached himself to 1 or 2 teammates, the insults were both brutal and unrelenting. As a result, I was proud, yet fearful when he said he was going to give football another try.

It was a beautiful day in September; I was picking Michael up from football practice. Football practice occurred every single day after school for 2 hours. I could see from the distress in his face that something had happened. During practice, one of the bigger players was going to throw an entire cooler of water at him. Michael had warned him, "Don't even think about it. If you do, you will regret it!" He threw the water and the cooler anyway. In response, Michael ran towards him, grabbed him by his front shoulder pads, threw him to the ground, and pushed his helmet into the dirt.

I was flabbergasted. Michael had pointed this same player out to me once. This kid was a big giant even without his equipment! When I finally found my voice, I told him I was pleased he had defended himself. However, Michael did not want to discuss the incident further: "Please don't be proud of what I did because I don't like treating anyone like that. I only did it because I had no choice." Apparently, my son, the boy who had been the long-suffering target of dozens of such bullies so many years ago, no longer existed. His coach assured me that Michael had handled himself very well. The following day, the coach informed me that the bully was going to run laps all during practice as punishment. I was elated that someone was finally being held responsible for their behavior.

It is very unfortunate that we still need to teach our children about the cruelty that continues to exist in the 21st century. As parents, we find ourselves forced to show them how to protect and defend themselves, even if it makes them uncomfortable to sink to that level of behavior. We need to remember that children are a product of their environment; the saying *"the apple doesn't fall far from the tree"* has some truth to it. As adults, we should first examine ourselves to make sure these behaviors are not being taught at home, whether consciously or unconsciously. Second, we should recognize that our children are not perfect angels and are capable of doing anything when not in our company. Third, and most importantly, we must learn and then teach our children to tolerate what is different in our society and not to judge others.

Chapter 2
"Take Me Out to the Ball Game"
Anthony Jr. is Playing Baseball

It was March 2013: My older son Anthony's behavior specialist and mentor called to tell me that a local baseball league had a division for special needs children. Anthony Jr. had always been passionate about baseball and his dream was finally about to come true. He would be in the Challenger Division Little League. My heart was dancing for him. Finally, he would get to experience what he loves most - with children who would accept him - and with coaches that have hearts of gold and saintly patience.

Anthony's first game was played in the second week in April. I made sure Grandma Angela marked it on her calendar so that we could go and support him on opening day. She was so excited for him that she began to cry. When that day came, my parents met us at the field.

The Challengers play ball unlike most Little League teams. There's no such thing as a strike or a ball; every player can stay at bat until they get a hit; they don't even keep score. However, when you see the players (most of whom have special needs) running around the bases on a beautiful Sunday morning, there's no doubt about it: score or no score, strikes or no strikes, they're having some good old-fashioned baseball fun.

Since its launch in 1998, the Little League Challengers have always been a non-competitive, co-ed league. While the players do get the opportunity to work on their batting and fielding skills, the emphasis is placed more upon providing the benefits of the team sports experience to those who have traditionally been denied it. The true goal is to bring special needs children out on the field to interact with other kids, to breathe some fresh air, and to have a real blast.

That first game in April, I remember it being quite chilly, but not cold enough to frost the warmth in our hearts. As we watched those children giving it their all and being part of a team with their friends, we could see their smiles and feel their excitement. I cannot put my emotions into words…you had to be there with me all the way to understand what this game meant to me. Anthony's hero is Derek Jeter, the New York Yankees shortstop for eighteen years and a five-time world champion. This he knows about…and now there he was, having his own "Jeter Moment!"

Anthony Jr. has some arm. He can really hit that ball into another dimension. It's so amazing to watch that you almost forget his disabilities. When I looked at him in his uniform that day, my spirits soared to see him so happy. When he hit the ball, it went over the fence into the parking lot. It was gone! I was wildly screaming at him to run the bases. He made it all the way to home plate! My son, my son, my son! How I love that boy!

For those of you who are fortunate enough to have a child participate in a sport, please understand that while winning is important, it isn't everything. If your child is trying his best, then that's what should matter. You should be elated that they are capable of understanding the game, following the rules, running on two legs, coordinating their bodies, and seeing, hearing, communicating, and doing all the things that parents of healthy children take for granted every day. Recognize that you received the gift of health through your children. Rejoice in your good fortune and don't ever take it for granted.

Chapter 3
"Out of the Mouths of Babes"
Hurricane Sandy

Thursday, October 22, 2012 felt a little different from any other day. I had this queasy, anxious feeling in the pit of my stomach that told me something was going to happen over which I would have absolutely no control. Over the years, we have had a multitude of dire forecasts of storms that somehow just missed Long Island, but now my intuition was telling me that this time was going to be quite different, and yes, as you all know, it certainly was.

The day was a routine one, yet strangely quiet. After I had completed my usual chores, the unsettled feelings I had experienced earlier in the day came rushing back over me. I knew it had to be my "second sense," which had been proven right time and time again. In the late afternoon, a weather alert had been issued regarding a super storm named "Sandy" that was making a steady path towards the tri-state area (New Jersey, Connecticut and Long Island). Despite having heard weather predictions like this before, my inner voice told me that Sandy was without question going to be "the big one."

I thought it best to keep my concerns to myself. I took some time to pray and asked whatever force that I was feeling to please keep my family safe from harm. These prayers sustained me, lightening the dread I had been experiencing; in its place stood safety and warmth. Now I was able to breathe easier, knowing that whatever was going to happen, my unwavering faith would protect us all.

My youngest son Michael arrived home from school at 3:30. He tossed his backpack on the dining room table, took off his jacket and shoes and, with his warm smile, asked how my day was and if everything was alright. His next question (not a surprise, given his large appetite) concerned snack time. I made him a sandwich, while he spoke with excited anticipation about the sixth grade Halloween Parade. This was his last year before graduating from elementary school. I kept my worried thoughts buried inside deep because I feared that things might not work out the way he thought. However, I was determined not to ruin Halloween for him, one of childhood's favorite memories, so I had hidden the costumes, accessories and candy in the basement as I had always done from the time I was a young mother.

That evening, as my husband and I ate dinner, I spoke of my concerns.

He reassured me that he would secure the house and not to worry so much because we live one mile from the water. I knew he was trying his best to calm me, but inside I was not sharing his confidence. While tossing and turning, trying to sleep, I was consumed by maternal instincts to pick up my son, Anthony Jr. who lives in a residence for special needs children. After all, he was not that far away and I wanted to keep him safe with us until the storm had passed.

Having made my decision, I drove Michael to school in the morning and then called Anthony's residence. I made sure that the medical office would know to give me enough medications until this unpredictable storm would finally end. It was vital that my family remain all together under one roof now.

I arrived at the residence where Anthony Jr. worriedly asked why I was picking him up so early on a Friday morning. This was not routine for him. Grandpa Armando and Grandma Angela usually came to get him on Friday afternoons. By this time, I had had enough life experience to know that my son would sense when things were outside of the norm. So I kissed and hugged him and told him I missed him so much that I wanted to spend a little extra time with him. He was OK with that response, but I could still feel his apprehension. Autistic children are quite capable of sensing heightened emotions around them.

We drove straight home; Anthony Jr. was extremely quiet. I gave him a snack and he became preoccupied with his iPad. He asked why our family dog Jake did not leave his cage and was acting as if he were afraid of something. I was once again astounded by how his keen observation of our dog told him that Jake was not himself that day. He looked at me for an explanation. Not wanting to scare him, I just said that Jake might be a little bit more tired than usual.

I then tried to change the subject, but Anthony pursued the topic by asking if I thought Jake knew about the big storm that was coming. I was flabbergasted that he had already become aware of "Super Storm Sandy." Years before, he would have not been able to communicate his concerns out loud. I asked him what he knew about the storm and he said with assurance, "It's going to be big, so we should make sure we take safety precautions for inside and outside our home, for the public to stay inside and, if your mayor or police tell you to leave your home, you leave!" At this point I was more than impressed with how completely Anthony realized the risks we might be facing.

Michael had just finished learning the consequences of bad weather in his sixth-grade science class: the measures you needed to take during hazardous storms and how to keep yourself and your family safe. If you know anything about Asperger children, you understand that the syndrome is all about listening and following the rules. So, it was no surprise to me when Michael came home from school that day with a list of things we needed to have in the house: flashlights with working batteries, lots of candles, lighters, canned food, a supply of water bottles, and a generator. By the end of the day, we were as prepared as we could be for what was to come. If it had not been so frightening, I would have felt like we were about to embark on a family adventure.

By Friday evening though, the sense of adventure had turned into something more sinister. To ward it off, we watched television and played a few board games. When it was time for bed, the boys went straight to their room. Around 10:00PM, it started to rain with some ordinary wind. Maybe it would not be that bad. However, in time, the rain had become tumultuous with fierce uncontrollable gusts. The boys were so frightened that they asked to spend the night in our bed. Jake was crying uncontrollably from his crate. He has a very even temperament, but you could actually hear his fear and distress as he whimpered. We let Jake into our bed and now our family was complete.

It was a night of fear, frustration, anxiety and stress. What would tomorrow bring? The worst was yet to come and my husband and I knew it. We tried to keep ourselves from the windows, but the howling of the wind and force of the torrents was so frightening that our curiosity sometime got the best of us. We ached to look outside like children, just to see what was going on.

Then, as our sons looked out of our front window, my neighbor's patio furniture flew over their home and landed in their front yard. We were trying to take all of this in when the phone rang: It was my neighbor Lynn. I immediately asked if they were alright. She explained that, while passing her front window, she saw our trampoline (which we thought had been secure enough) fly over the fence and that it was now making its way down the block, rolling on its side. My husband threw on his boots and jacket to help her husband hold onto the trampoline. Then our neighbor Paul, the one who had just lost his patio furniture, ran to help us with his tools. Paul made a quick decision to chop the trampoline into pieces before it damaged property or, even worse, hurt someone.

Anthony Jr. looked at me and said, "Mommy, we have no control over what's going on outside, only God does." I was having the exact same thought, but he said it aloud… *out of the mouths of babes.* No sooner had he made his pronouncement, we lost all power to our home. We had a radio but could only listen to the news that the water was rising in certain areas of our beloved town.

I became consumed with worry for my brother because he lived on the south shore near the rising waters. I had faith that he was prepared, but this storm seemed to have an uncontrollable vengeance and I had heard about serious flooding in his area. We had sporadic cell phone service throughout the night, which was very frustrating. Afterwards we found out that he protected his home and family like a true warrior, pumping the water out of his basement throughout the stormy night.

The next day was Sunday; Sandy was gone, but much remained to be done. The destruction and emotional upheaval that this storm left behind was enormous. When you were finally able to drive around, it was difficult to take in all that had happened. It was surreal and quite unbelievable. Our home had no real damage, but we felt horrible for the people who had lost everything or who had had damage to their homes. We were so grateful that we were all safe, including all our family members and close friends.

My boys wanted to know how we could help the community and those in need. We shopped and bought much needed supplies for the elementary school and our church. Our donation consisted of twelve bags of everyday supplies, such as toiletries, canned food, water, etc... Michael looked at me and said it really felt good to give and help others. I made sure that my children knew just how close we came to being in the same situation.

Despite my enormous sense of fear, I have never felt so very close to God's presence. I had learned firsthand that we are not in total command of our lives. As humans, we would like to believe we can control things, but it is God who has full mastery and may have other plans for us. We lost power for an entire week and for the most part, it was nice to be separated from outside technology, playing board games and having conversations via candlelight. We cherished this special time of being a traditional family, of putting things into perspective, and of realizing what was really important to us. Life is too short to have regrets, so live every day as if it were your last. It is my fervent hope that most of us will walk away from this experience with a lesson or two learned because it the hardest of times that molds our character and defines who we truly are.

Chapter 4
"DO I KNOW THAT BOY?"
Why My Family?

August 20, 2012 started off like any other day. Anthony had stayed with us for an extended weekend. (Anthony usually resided with us on weekends. Now age thirteen, Anthony has been out of our home since he was eight years old.) The alarm sounded at 7AM and I could hear the birds softly chirping outside my window. With the sun shining into my bedroom, warming me inside and out, I said under my breath, "What a beautiful day…" Quietly taking my steps ever so lightly around my home so as not to awaken my sleeping boys, I tried to get myself ready for whatever the day might bring.

Just as quickly as the sun hides behind a cloud, my mind went on high alert when, on the other side of my bedroom door, I heard a familiar refrain: "Mommy - it's Anthony - I'm hungry!" Before I could respond, he galloped into the kitchen, seeking out whatever food was readily available, but he was soon distracted by the plaintive yelping of our dog Jake who wanted desperately to be let out of his crate. Anthony nobly released him, but neglected to open the back door, which was crucial for Jake's physical needs. Instead, Anthony repeated his "I'm-hungry!!!" mantra without stopping. His Obsessive-Compulsive Disorder was now in full gear and it was not even 8:00 am yet.

I needed to immediately tend to my son due to his prescribed regimen of medications. I carefully handed him his cocktail of meds in a medication cup. I turned aside to prepare sunny-side up eggs, with well-done bacon and home fries. As I turned to hand Anthony his favorite breakfast, he threw the cup of meds at me. I was now shaking with anger as I knelt on the floor gathering and counting pills, "one, two, three, four, five six, seven, eight," shaking my head, holding my breath, and asking myself, "Why me, why my family?"

While picking myself up off the floor, I heard him asking me for ketchup for the fifth time. He had finished his breakfast, taken his pills from my hands one by one, and had run without warning out the front door. This is a typical day in the life of a family dealing with the toxic combination of autism and raging teenage hormones. His neurologist had warned me that there would be a long string of days like this once puberty had set in. Anthony's complete menu of diagnoses includes: Pervasive Developmental Disorder, Attention Deficit Hyperactivity Disorder, Obsessive Compulsive traits, Oppositional Defiance, Anxiety, Depression and Epilepsy.

Back at home, my neighbors across the way were listening and staring at the commotion taking place. Of course, I wanted to hide under a rock from complete embarrassment, weary of yet another odd episode at our household. Under my breath, I was thinking that I just wanted all of this to go away. I hadn't signed up for this.

My younger son Michael was awakened by my screams that had been set off by Anthony running into the street throwing rocks at our front glass door as well as the windows. With his all-too-familiar look of despair, my younger boy asked, "Mom, are you alright?" We both went outside and began the ritual of calming Anthony down. In response, he took off his shirt, hurled it at me, and shrieked, "Leave me alone!" Feeling helpless, I asked him what was wrong. In the middle of throwing rocks at parked cars, he suddenly stopped, raised his head to look at me and confessed what I already knew about him deep down inside of my soul: "I want to be good. I don't know why I do what I do."

Before I could stop him, Anthony ran around the corner, in front of my neighbors' home. They are more like my guardian angels, if you ask me. From their front window, I heard a soft voice: "Anthony, please behave. Listen to your mom. She loves you. You're going to get hurt. We don't want anything to happen to you."

Michael grabbed hold of his brother, as Anthony continued to kick, shove and bite in protest. I was trying desperately to get them both away from the traffic in the street and back into the safety and privacy of home. My hands and body were shaking uncontrollably. Why do my neighbors always have to know my business? I was totally mortified and just wanted to hide out for the day. I just wanted this clown show to end.

In the front door hallway laid a pool of urine from my dog Jake. Luckily, this was not normal and only happened when he was stressed. As I searched through the house for Jake, I saw his light beige tail sticking out from under my bed. I wondered if there was room for me under there.

As I turned my head, I could see Anthony out of the corner of my eye. He was hitting himself in the head. I clutched his hands and kissed his face: "Do you have any idea how much I love you? Please stop hurting yourself. I don't want anything to happen to you. Lie down on your bed, think about what just happened and the consequences for your actions." These words have become my mantra far more often than I care to admit.

It's only 9:00 am, but it was obvious at this point that I was going to need outside help. So, I tearfully called in my support team, my parents, who could hear the frustration and panic in my voice. As always, they immediately understood what needed to be done. Fifteen minutes later the doorbell rang, both to my sorrow and my relief. It was my heroes who have come to whisk Anthony away and give me a much-needed break.

I looked out my window as the car drove away, with Michael at my side. "Why is he like that, Mom? It's really hard when he comes home because I feel responsible for him even though he's older than me." His questions made me examine my own role as a parent. Why couldn't I handle the situation as I knew I should, without having to rely on my parents? And the even bigger accusation: Why do I always feel so guilty?

So, resuming my parental responsibility now that Anthony was out of the way, I reminded Michael of his brother's disabilities. As an eleven-year-old with a recent diagnosis of Asperger's Syndrome, Michael was finding it increasingly difficult to comprehend and deal with his own struggles, much less those of his older brother.

Afterwards, I sat at my kitchen table, holding a wet tissue in one hand and a stale cup of coffee in the other. To think I had awakened early to take care of myself, say a few prayers, and have a few minutes of quality time. What was I thinking?

The morning quickly disappeared; it was time to retrieve Anthony for his 2:30PM neurology appointment. As I drove along with the top down on my Mustang, the stagnant coffee started to churn inside of me, twisting my insides into tangles of knots as I relived the morning's events. When I saw him, he was blissfully unaware of what had gone on just a few short hours ago. I thanked God for small miracles.

We arrived at the neurologist's office at 2:15PM for his routine check-up. Bad news: the doctor was running extremely late due to a new the restroom. After a while, I realized that he had been in there too long. I knocked quietly at the door and heard "I need you, Mom." I looked into the toilet and saw a huge pool of blood. He had torn his anal fissure because of difficult bowel movements caused by his medications. In a moment, he was crying in my arms in the restroom, telling me he was so sorry for making me sad and for being the way he was. I cleaned him up and hoped this awful day would not get any worse.

Both my children were now very hungry and frustrated because of the interminable wait. We were seen approximately 45 minutes later, only to receive a refill on prescriptions. The visit was a rushed one without any sense of accomplishment. Why make any child wait this long? Thank God Grandma Angela had given us some leftover food that was in the trunk of my car. There's nothing quite like homemade pizza, fresh oven baked bread, frittata (egg vegetable pie), fried meatballs and some iced tea to wash it down. Who needed a drive-through?!

We drove Anthony back to his "other home" and another wave of unbearable sadness washed over me, caused by the guilt of leaving him behind, the sadness of the morning, and the constant heartbreak of a special needs parent. What does he think at night when he's lying in his bed alone? Does he think we abandoned him?

On the homebound drive I could not help thinking about what his future would have been like if he had been born neurotypical. *Would he have been playing sports? Would he have had sleepovers? Would he have had a best friend to confide in? Would he have shared that special bond that only brothers have? What could have been for me and my family?* Why do I keep torturing myself with these *would-have / could-have / should-have* scenarios?

It was now evening; I was lying in bed emotionally exhausted, and I could not sleep. I tried to pray, but my guilt continued to eat at me. I kept asking myself, "Who was that boy in the street this morning? Am I really his mother? Was a mistake made somehow? Am I doing everything that I can for him?" All this is just too overwhelming to carry inside on a daily basis. What made it more impossible to deal with was the combination of his perfectly beautiful angelic face with his unexpected and frightening outbursts of fury. Strangers would never know how this sweet boy was trapped inside a body of disarray and confusion. My final thought was that this awful day really needed to come to an end so that the sun could rise again tomorrow.

Chapter 5
"Hello, is Michael Home?"
The Invention

My alarm went off - it's 8:00 am. I slowly awakened to "What a Wonderful World" by Louis Armstrong. Its melody and lyrics made me appreciate the beauty and hope that a new day always inspired in me.

As I sprang out of bed and placed my feet on the hardwood floor, I noticed that one of my slippers was missing. The only culprit I could think of was Jake, who I was sure had hidden it among his belongings. Sure enough, as I lifted the blanket off his crate, I could see a small patch of my fuzzy black slipper under his beige curly hair as he slept. He was sleeping so peacefully that I decided to leave him be. If having one slipper would be the worst part of my day, I could handle it.

It was the beginning of summer 2012, and what a hot day it promised to be. On the morning news, the weather forecast predicted temperatures in the high 90's, with the possibility of reaching 100 degrees. I decided to spend the day at the town pool. As I prepared the cooler with ice, made sandwiches, packed drinks, found snacks in the cupboard, and stuffed it all, along with the towels and sun block, into the beach bag, it was time for a second cup of coffee.

As I sat in deep thought wondering what Anthony would be doing for the day at his residence, my phone rang. The very professional voice on the other end asked to speak with Michael.

"He's sleeping at the moment. May I ask who is calling?"

"This is Meghan Walters from the Dannison Corporation."

I was now bewildered and curious: "Is there something I can help you with? I'm his mother."

"Yes, I would like to discuss his email and video correspondence regarding his invention that he submitted to our corporation."

Shocked and speechless, I told her that Michael was only 11 years old. Meghan asked that a conference call be arranged at our earliest convenience to discuss his submission, his ideas on design, the chain of prototyping, obtaining a patent, and ultimately marketing the product to corporations. She then informed me that I would need to represent him because of his age. Wondering if this is some sort of prank, I told her I would call her back.

I reached for my iPad to search for Dannison Corporation, only to find out it was one of the largest patent invention companies in the United States.

WHAT? Could this be? As I scratched my head in disbelief, I decided it was time to wake up Michael to find out more about this mysterious phone call.

In a loud singing voice I called, "Michael - rise and shine!"

In a groggy voice, he murmured, "What time is it?"

"It's 10:30 - time for you to wake up!" He gave me his familiar one-eye-open-yawning-sleepy- head look.

With a smirk on my face, I asked "Did you submit a video and email to the Dannison Corporation about an invention?"

"Yes, I did. What's for breakfast?"

Michael went into the bathroom, leaving me just as confused as I was when I first received the telephone call. He then sat at the kitchen table and asked me:

"Mom, I thought I heard the phone ring. Who was that? May I have pancakes?"

"The answers to your questions are: Meghan Walters from the Dannison Corporation about your invention, and yes, you may have pancakes. Now I have a question for you, What invention Michael?"

"I asked you the other day how an idea for a new product could be turned into something that could be sold to the public. You told me the internet usually has companies that could help submit ideas to present to a corporation. So I did my research, introduced myself by email, sent my idea by video, and that's why she's calling. Good old technology, Ma."

Totally taken aback, I told him we needed to call her back to set up a future conference call because of his age. He had apparently taken care of that legality already by informing her in that first email that I would be representing him.

After breakfast, Michael decided he would call her back to discuss the project further. By this time, I'm on my third cup of coffee, wondering in disbelief if this was really happening and not just one of my more pleasant dreams. My anticipation was getting ahead of me.

It had to be the first time I had ever seen Michael eat so slowly. I recall asking myself if he was really eating that slowly or was it that I lacked the patience to wait for him to make this phone call. Then he had the nerve to ask for seconds!

I looked at him sternly. "You need to make that call! Aren't you the least bit curious about all this?"

He laughed, looked me straight in the eye and said, "No, she can wait."

"If you want more pancakes, you will make that phone call now!"

That did the trick! He dialed the number and put it on speaker. We heard that same lovely voice of Meghan Walters, Vice President of New Products of Dannison Corporation:

"Your invention has been reviewed by our staff; we are interested in your idea and would like to expand it further. Since you are one of the youngest inventors ever to submit an idea, we will be working closely with you and your mother. We will be sending you a copy of the Dannison Corporation Confidentiality Agreement. When you receive the documents by email, please sign them, fax them back to our corporate office, and then we will set up a conference call to discuss the process further on a future date."

After the phone call, he calmly requested yet another serving of pancakes. At that moment, I was still focused on the conference call that just had taken place.

He looked over at me and announced, "Cool…right? What are we doing today?"

"Michael, I thought we would go to the pool since it's going to be a hot day."

As I handed him another helping and he poured syrup over the pancakes, I was acutely aware that the morning's events hadn't fazed him in the least. This was Asperger's Syndrome at its finest.

An hour later we received the confidentiality agreement by email. We reviewed the document together, page after page. With pride and a great big smile, Michael signed his name. "Mom can you please fax this back for me?" I asked him if I worked for him now. "Yes, you do….I'm on my way to becoming an entrepreneur!"

Chapter 6
"Miracles Do Happen"
The EEG

It was March 1, 2012 around 6:00 am. I was exhausted from having to keep Anthony Jr. awake the night before for today's EEG at the hospital. An EEG (electroencephalogram) is a test that measures and records the electrical activity of your brain by using sensors (electrodes) attached to your head. We sleep-deprive him so that he can stay calm and reach sleep mode while in the hospital bed as the technician monitors him. It is a nerve-wracking experience- before, during and afterwards. Before — because it is emotionally, mentally, and physically debilitating for us to stay awake, knowing what was to come the next day. During — because it is so hard to watch your child go through it all, knowing how scary it must seem to him. After — because we have to wait by the phone every day, dreading to hear the results. Yet, we have had to accept this ordeal every six months since Anthony was first diagnosed with epilepsy at the age of three and have come to accept it as part of our family routine.

Why was I so tired? Well, my husband can sleep through just about anything, which left me flying solo during the torturous process of sleep-depriving our son. During the night I found myself asking "Who is really being tortured here — Anthony or me?" He thinks of it as one big party with no set bedtime. Despite my having consumed two cups of coffee and a huge bucket of buttered popcorn, I still struggled to keep my eyes open while watching Harry Potter's *The Half Blood Prince* and *The Deathly Hallows* movies. Anthony finally fell asleep at 2:00 am, but then I could not sleep at all, as on many other nights in the life of a mother with a special needs child.

Almost comatose, I sleepwalked into my son's room the next morning and watched him slumbering like an angel. I gazed up at the ceiling, asking for strength, patience and most of all, some positive news.

I kissed him on his forehead and told him, "Sorry buddy, I know you're tired, but today's the day."

He gave me his drowsy-but-determined look. "I'm taking Yoda with me to keep me company while I take my test."

I told him what was always in my heart, "You are the bravest boy in the entire world and such a trooper! Yoda and Luke Skywalker will never be as brave as you."

With a great big smile, he rose out of bed, kissed me on the cheek, asked for help getting dressed, and told me he was starving (as usual).

I needed to scurry now, rushing to wash my face, brush my teeth, fix my hair, and apply a fast lick of lipstick. Running into my bedroom, I passed my husband in the hallway and realized that he was not only ready to leave, but that he had already had his coffee! He reminded me what I already knew…that I had 15 minutes to get ready and out the door. He made another familiar pronouncement: "What's taking you so long?" Don't you just love men? Here is where my patience must kick in. Counting to ten, I calmly instructed him, "Please go to the Indian Chief Deli and pick up egg sandwiches to eat in the car, since you seem to have more time than me."

Once I heard the front door close, I put on my shoes, took my medications and remembered to let Jake out for his "morning constitutional." While he was outside, I filled up his bowls with water and dog food. Next, I needed to give Anthony Jr. his medications. As I heard Jake barking, my husband rang the front doorbell with the egg sandwiches in one hand and coffee in the other. I checked my purse to make sure I had his written prescription, our insurance card and enough quarters for the meter in front of the hospital. Anthony was dragging Yoda out the front door, followed by my husband. I was left to lock up.

We arrived at the admitting desk around 7:30 am for his 9:00 am appointment. While we were waiting to be called, I took some time for morning prayers. As I was about to finish, I heard them call my son's name. The administrator intoned, "You know the procedure - all paperwork needs to be filled out before we proceed to the Neurology Department."

Although we had done this on a number of occasions, I had knots in my stomach and an instant tension headache, most likely from sleep deprivation. The EEG technician greeted us, glanced at Anthony's hospital bracelet, and said, "Room 404." My son was holding Yoda tightly, but he resolutely climbed onto the hospital bed. Before closing his eyes, he assured me in a soft whisper, "Mom, it's going to be OK." The technician asked him to lay still while he glued approximately 20 electrodes to his head and then wrapped it with gauze in the shape of a hat. This allowed the technician to look at his brain activity from the monitor. Since it was an ambulatory EEG, we were able to take him home with a portable electroencephalogram to observe any seizure activity throughout the day, at night, and during sleep. While he slept in our bedroom, my husband and I took turns monitoring him.

The next morning, Anthony tapped me on the shoulder at 7:00 am after his special night of watching movies, playing board games, reading books, and being given back rubs and leg massages. He enjoys leg massages the most because of the cramps he gets from the seizure medication. Of course, he wanted the electrodes out of his head immediately. "Please Mom- now!" At the kitchen table, I realized he had gathered a plastic bag for the electrodes, nail polish remover, and cotton to remove the glue, and a separate bag for the electroencephalogram. In a nanosecond, it dawned on me how grown up he had become.

He sat expectantly at the kitchen table, waiting for me to begin the familiar procedure. After the first seven electrodes had been removed, he demanded in a very loud and annoyed voice, "How much longer?" This question was repeated until after the tenth and final time, when I was able to finally say, "OK - all done." He sighed loudly, "Holy crap, Mom, that's freaking torture!" It is important to remember that Anthony was a child that had had an 80% processing delay and could barely put full sentences together only a few years ago. Now he was able to put entire sentences together and use select curse words (if not all) in proper formation. I never thought I would be able to describe my oldest son as a typical teenager.

At this point, my husband needed to return all the testing data and material to the hospital in order for Anthony's EEG report to be read by his neurologist. We usually do not get the results back for at least seven to ten days, if not longer. However, I was in no hurry to yet again be told that his EEG was still showing spikes continuously throughout his day and while sleeping. Over the years, his EEG results have never showed any signs of improvement.

On March 13th, the neurologist called me with the results. She said the EEG showed no spike activity during the day, only while sleeping. I took a deep breath and asked, "Excuse me, can you please repeat that?" Her voice swelled with satisfaction as she repeated, "I am happy to inform you that there have been significant improvements with his brain activity throughout the day." She went on to explain that he could also, in time, outgrow the abnormal spike activity during sleep once his body went through puberty and his brain was fully developed.

After hearing these unexpectedly positive results, I became so emotional that I could barely breathe or speak. I quickly called my husband to give him the good news. He choked up and could not believe what I was telling him. Knowing in my heart that his feelings as Anthony's parent could only mirror those of my own, I was certain he was tearing up. I always knew my husband suffered silently because of our child's disabilities. Yet, he was unable to voice his inner disappointment and worries for his son's future out loud. Holding back tears, he softly told me, "Honey, I love you - talk to you when I get home."

My next step was to call the rest of my family and friends with the wonderful and hopeful news. After all the calls were made, in the midst of all the excitement, I remembered that I needed to prepare dinner. Thank God for Grandma Angela, who had given me some sauce with meatballs. All I needed to do was boil the ravioli. My younger son Michael and I ate dinner, made a plate for my husband, checked Michael's homework, and prepared him for school the next day.

My husband walked in at the usual time, hugged me and said, "I know I don't tell you often enough, but you're a great mom! I guess miracles do happen. Thanks for always having faith, having patience, and being positive in what sometimes seems to be a hopeless situation." I was beginning to think that maybe, just maybe everything was going to be OK.

Chapter 7
Knowing When You Need Help and Knowing When to Ask For It"
My Appointment With J. Lo

When Anthony Jr. left our home, it was one of the darkest moments in my life. I remember sleeping with his light blue bunny sweater under my pillow. I cut one off one of the rabbit ears on the hood so I could carry it in my pocketbook. I would cry in the shower every morning so that no one would know my heart's devastation. My daily ritual became lying on the bed in a fetal position, crying until I had no more tears left, and remaining like that for hours on end. The truth was that I was unable to sleep unless I took something at night to help me. My own parents and brother were at odds with my decision and the separation from them broke my heart. I was slowly dying inside, but it was crucial that I get my act together for my son Michael and my husband Anthony.

My neighbor and friend Laura urged me to go for counseling. She explained how sometimes in life, no matter how strong you think you are, you need a professional to help you cope with this thing called "depression." I felt like nothing was important anymore; I was so tired and so sad that just getting out of bed was difficult. I was not really living; I was simply surviving.

When I met the social worker for my first appointment, I knew she would become a good friend. She instinctively understood how I felt and empathized with what I was going through: my struggles and worries as a parent over my sons' futures, my gut-wrenching guilt over moving Anthony Jr. out of our home, the increasing distance between my husband and me, and my anger as a parent of a disabled child. From her, I learned that forgiveness can be a very powerful tool in the healing process. Once you are able to forgive yourself and others, you can experience something called "peace within your heart."

I continued to see her for a couple of months, and then she introduced me to a clinical psychiatrist. He immediately impressed me because he focused on the real issues, spoke truthfully and did not waste my time. Not only was he a good listener, but he also gave sound advice. He said that what I was going through was "normal," but that I was like a train going full speed ahead with no brakes. Sooner or later, I was either going to crash or run out of fuel.

He told me that "sometimes in life we a need a little help - and it's alright to ask for it." This would not be easy for me because I had always helped myself and did everything on my own. In other words, I was Miss Independence! He assured me that supervised medication would help me overcome my depression and so he prescribed Zoloft, which shortly made me feel myself again. What a huge difference it made!

These sessions of self-discovery led me to realize that when a mother has an unconditional love for her child, she is capable of putting her child 's needs before her own. I also discovered that the acceptance of your child's disabilities is the key to accepting help when you need it, and that difficult choices do not come without consequences. The hardest lesson I had to learn was to forgive myself and others in order to achieve an inner peace.

However, I also learned that the path I had chosen was not an easy one for me, my husband, or those around me. I can now say that this ongoing experience definitely strengthened my human spirit and gave me the insight to recognize my choices as steppingstones towards a healthy family. The emotional pain cultivated an inner strength to become a leader and a voice for those children who cannot speak for themselves. Yet, although my intuition insisted that I needed to make this unselfish decision, that feeling alone did not make it all OK.

For those of you who struggle to raise your special children and feel it is nobler to suffer in silence, remember you are not alone on your journey. You have partners, i.e., other parents in the same situation. Please reach out to those parents and don't be afraid to admit you need professional help to live with your heartache.

Chapter 8
"If it Looks Like a Bully and Acts Like a Bully, It's a Bully!" The Bus Ride Showdown

June 10th, 2011 started off like any other day. Michael's alarm rang at 8:00 am; he washed his face, brushed his teeth, dressed, and ate his breakfast. He was so excited because school was almost out for the summer. He was in 4th grade at our local elementary school. The bus pulled up to our home at approximately 9:05 am that morning.

However, despite the seeming normalcy of his morning routine, since March, Michael had been coming home emotionally distraught from numerous incidences that had been occurring on the bus ride to and from school. I reported it to the bus driver, the principal and vice principal, only to have my complaints fall on deaf ears. The principal's plan consisted of calling *"trustworthy children that always tell the truth"* into her office, and then accepting their stories as fact. Fearful of repercussions and losing their jobs, the bus monitors would not defend my son during these attacks. These bullies consisted of eight students in the 6th, 5th, 4th and 3rd graders that would call Michael awful names, as well as hitting, punching, and cursing at him. This behavior was allowed to continue every day from early March up to mid-June. The abuse was everywhere: while Michael boarded the bus, exited the bus, walked in the hallways, and had recess on the playground.

I decided it was time to take matters into my own hands. We purchased an iPhone that could take clear video and record voices. I instructed Michael to start recording whenever he felt threatened, whether it was cursing, hitting, or something worse. On a number of occasions, he would call me from the bus and ask me to listen. It was awful to have to hear firsthand what my son was going through, but at least now I knew I would have the proof I needed to go forward.

My stomach would churn every time I saw him board that accursed bus. I longed to defend Michael because, as parents, our instincts are to protect our children. Yet, I also knew that eventually he would have to learn to defend himself. Each day, I anxiously waited at the bus stop, not knowing in what condition Michael would arrive home. This particular day, he ran off the bus in hysterics, unable to breathe or finish his sentences. He made his way up my front stairs, pulled up his shirt and showed me an angry bruise in the shape of a boot heel on his upper left stomach area. I became enraged!

In the midst of all the hysteria, the vice principal called. She began the conversation by telling me she had just received a disturbing phone call from the parent of a second grader who reported that Michael pushed him on the bus today.

Given my mood at the time, my knee-jerk response was, "You need to get your story straight because it was my son who was kicked in the stomach by that same 2nd grader! What's more, I have photos and videotapes of all of the bullying that has been carried out on that bus against Michael. My husband and I will be in your office at 9:00 am tomorrow to show you the photos of his latest bruise as well as other photos and videotape. Enough is enough! These incidents must stop. As you well know, this abuse has been going on since March of this year."

When my husband arrived home that night, I knew that I needed to remain calm while I related to him what had happened. If I could not keep my emotions in check, my husband would definitely be out-of-control at the school. I prayed for calmness and the ability to somehow ease my surging anger. I knew that I would need my total inner strength for the battle ahead of me. We let Michael sleep in our room, but it was a fitful sleep accompanied by night sweats, anxiety attacks, nightmares, and downright fear of what would happen to him on the bus and at school the next day. This would be the one of many such nights that we would have to endure until the situation would be finally resolved.

The next day he stayed home. In good conscience, I could not permit him to step foot in that school until someone was held accountable for what had taken place on that bus. My husband and I entered the principal's office, and were greeted by her, the vice-principal, and the Superintendent of Transportation. Of course, I was prepared for the typical bureaucratic response to all parental complaints: The bus driver was not responsible because she had to keep her eyes on the road; the transportation company was not responsible because they are contracted outside the school; the school was not responsible because the bullying happened off school grounds. My response could only be: "WHAT?"

We then played the videotape for them at full volume. I could not even bear to watch it. A single tear ran down my cheek and for once, I was actually speechless. They suggested separating Michael by having him sit in the front of the bus, while the bullies sat in the back. I argued that that would be victimizing the victim. Next, they suggested that his bus be changed, which meant that the school authorities were either unwilling or unable to change the bullying situation. Their only solutions were to change Michael's seat or his bus.

The absurdity was such that I demanded that the parents of the students shown bullying on the videotape be notified of the occurrence and be held responsible their children's actions. The extent of their response to the situation was only that the child who kicked my son would be taken off that bus and not be allowed to attend any year end festivities. I then questioned the bus driver's experience, inaction, and negligence in stopping the bus while my son was being assaulted. They repeated the same excuses I had heard earlier. Since I felt this meeting was getting us nowhere, I requested an immediate meeting with the superintendent of our school district.

At this point, despite my being emotionally exhausted, I was mentally preparing myself for the next strategic step. I would do whatever it would take to protect Michael because to see him like this was killing me inside. It was time for a quiet prayer for guidance. My faith is my secret weapon. It strengthens me not only for battles such as this, but also helps me to live this life in a spiritual way for the sake of myself and my family.

After praying, my next step was to give my body a bit of pampering in the form of a mani-pedi at my favorite nail salon. As I relaxed in the pedicure chair, a friend I hadn't seen in a while sat next to me. We began to catch up with each other's lives and I felt I could share my current crisis with her. Without getting into details, I gave her a summary of Michael's ordeal. A longtime active advocate for her two children, she advised me to contact a firm she knew that provided professional advocacy services for children and their parents to obtain the programs and services that best meet the needs of the child. I felt that an angel in disguise had sat down next to me that day to have a pedicure. She provided me with the information I needed to put me on the right path to help my son.

When I returned home, I made my phone call to the agency. My angel was right; these ladies were not only knowledgeable, but they also brought a fresh perspective. I was aware that I was too closely involved to see things clearly. I needed their expertise and professional support; I asked them to attend the school district meeting with me.

During the conversation, I provided details about the bus incidents as well as the school's response. I described Michael's social "blindness," along with his inability to understand certain everyday situations or read body language and interact socially. She asked me if I had ever heard of Asperger's Syndrome. When she said those words, something clicked inside of me. How I cried on the phone! It was as if she knew my son better than I did. For some time, I had been tormented by the fear that something was amiss with my child, a fear that is hidden deeply inside of every parent and often disregarded. Asperger's Syndrome/Autism Spectrum Disorder (ASD) is characterized by significant difficulties in social interaction, alongside of restricted and repetitive patterns of behavior and interests. It differs from other autism spectrum disorders by its relative preservation of linguistic and cognitive development. Although not required for diagnosis, physical clumsiness and atypical use of language are frequently reported. Since I had one child under the Autism Spectrum, it made sense to have the other tested, especially when the siblings are boys. I should have known better.

The following day, I had a spiritual breakdown, which is very different from an emotional one. I was going to go food shopping, but I made a detour into the parking lot of my parish. I believed that speaking to a priest and asking why this would happen twice in one family would help me sort through my feelings of despair and isolation. After all, I had one child with Pervasive Developmental Disorder/Autism that I heartbreakingly surrendered to an agency residence and now I feared that my younger son had Asperger's Syndrome. I spoke to the priest, who listened intently and gave me a mother's blessing. He asked me to read the "Footprints in the Sand Prayer." Afterwards, I came to realize that I was truly not suffering alone or in silence, but that I was being carried on my journey with my children. We prayed together; I cried for two hours straight, scratching the corneas of my eyes with my contacts. Yet, believe it or not, I did feel an amazing peace come over me.

I was now prepared for the meeting, emotionally, spiritually, and mentally. A few days prior to the meeting, Michael had been tested, observed and diagnosed by a child psychologist, with not only with having Asperger's Syndrome, but also as emotionally disturbed by the bullying, which led to his having Post Traumatic Stress Disorder (PTSD). Now I could present this medical confirmation to my school district.

Our meeting date with the school district took place in the superintendent's offices. We had downloaded the bus video onto a computer screen. As we entered the boardroom, it was so quiet that one could hear the proverbial pin drop. Both advocates sat down to face the panel. One would type the meeting notes on her iPad as the other introduced the important topics of discussion. Seated at the table were the Superintendent of Transportation, the District Office Counsel, the Superintendent of Academics, the Assistant Superintendent, and the principal.

After listening to my complaints and utter disappointment at the lack of action taken on my son's behalf, the office counsel asked me, "Since there are only two more weeks left of school, what do you expect us to do at this late date?" She then pointed to the number of people at the meeting as proof of their concern. I pointed out that my concerns were first introduced back in March but had not been taken seriously until matters had escalated to such a point that I had no recourse but to take this next step.

After viewing the video of the assault, the transportation superintendent's opinion was that my son had provoked the altercation with his iPhone. He felt that the children were agitated because they did not want to be videotaped. I took a deep breath and pointed out that criminals also do not want to be videotaped when they are committing a crime. I went on, "Would you prefer that he bring a gun instead of an iPhone to school for protection? I am using the same skills I learned from working on Wall Street to protect my son…a clear, well-conceived strategy to achieve my ultimate goal – a safe environment for the students. I should think that goal would be shared by the school administrators as well!" As I expected, my argument silenced his ignorance.

Towards the end of the meeting, the advocates requested a private bus for my son, adding that we would get back to them with a full list of requests. More importantly, they instructed the educational administrators on how bullying could be handled without victimizing the victim. In closing, they gave a subtle, yet clear message, which was that our intention was to keep this episode private because we felt that the parents living in that district would not be comfortable with the way in which their children were being transported to and from school. They finished by advising the education officials that they would soon be hearing from us. I felt not only vindicated by what had transpired, but also confident in the team of advocates by my side. I no longer felt alone.

When I came home, my son Michael looked at me and said, "Mom it feels great to know you always have my back. That school now knows that you are no pushover! I love you, Mom." He then gave me a big bear hug, followed by "Mom you're the best!" It was all the reward I needed and would serve to sustain me for the struggles yet to come.

Chapter 9
"Our Family Vacation to Disney World"
Where Dreams Really Do Come True!

Oh, happy day… Disney here we come! Our goal as a family was to take a well- deserved family trip to Orlando when Anthony had reached his IEP (individual education plan) goals. His dream was to go to Universal Studios to visit the Wizardly World of Harry Potter. That day had finally arrived and I started to make vacation plans.

Our first step was to fly to Orlando, Florida. During the security check-in, we needed to remove our shoes before walking through the detectors. My son Anthony refused to take off his shoes, arguing that he had nothing hidden in them, but that he would remove his shoes if the airport security attendant removed his as well. He insisted that "It was a stupid law and that his feet did not smell!" It is difficult enough to explain this procedure to children (and even some adults!) that do not have special needs but imagine having to justify this odd ritual to a child with autism. We needed to pull Anthony aside and have a compassionate security screener spell out why he needed to remove his shoes. What finally convinced him to go along with the instructions was the fact that if he did not, we could not go to Disney to meet Mickey Mouse and all of his friends.

We finally arrived in Orlando's airport and next we needed to locate the Disney Express, which would take us and our luggage to our hotel. We had decided it would be best to stay at the Polynesian Resort so that we could be near the Disney tram in case of an emergency. The heat in Florida during the summer months is so intense and we were concerned that Anthony would suffer from heat exhaustion or seizures. The Polynesian Resort, with its two spectacular pools and landscaping of shady palm trees, was an absolutely perfect oasis for us. The only problem was that my husband had no sense of direction and so he kept getting lost going to and from our room. On the other hand, Michael has an incredible photogenic memory and sense of direction. My husband was constantly becoming frustrated by the fact he was always walking in circles; the more Michael tried to teach him the correct route, the madder he would become. It was so bad that he would tip the staff on the golf carts to drive us to and from the tram!

Anthony's face at Harry Potter's Amusement Park was priceless. His reaction made us believe along with him that we were in the presence of real wizards and warlocks. It is an amazing place to visit if you are a Harry Potter fanatic like Anthony. We spent the entire day at Universal Studios enjoying all the rides, drinking Butter Beer, and eating lunch at The Three Broomsticks.

I appreciated the staff's kindness and expertise in their interaction with special needs children. They gave us family fast passes because of the disabilities, which meant that we didn't have to wait on the seemingly endless lines in the heat, but instead were given access to a secret entrance. How cool is that!

The next day we visited Disney's Magic Kingdom (what an appropriate name for that place!) We were having lunch to celebrate Michael's belated birthday when suddenly Snow White and her Seven Dwarfs knocked on the glass window and asked the boys if they wanted to play hopscotch. Anthony was definitely not going to miss out on playing hopscotch with characters he'd always dreamed of meeting. If that wasn't enough of a dream-come-true experience, along came Cinderella and Little Bo Peep to join in the game. He couldn't believe his eyes! My heart danced with happiness knowing that he was so excited and happy. Autism did not exist for that one magical moment.

After lunch we decided to go back to the hotel for a well needed nap, planning to return for the Electric Parade that night. Unable to find his way to the right exit, my husband became exasperated. Michael coolly explained to his father that we were in the back of the Magic Kingdom Castle and that we just needed to go to the front, and then follow the brick path to the exit. It was hysterical to see my husband sitting on a bench, worn out by exhaustion, acting like a big kid who just wants to go home because he's tired of being lost. I remembered how concerned I was about our children having meltdowns, but it was my husband who became overwhelmed, overheated, and confused by all the outside stimulation. I had to smile inside.

Despite my husband's temporary regression, we all had a wonderful and unforgettable family trip. Most people expect to encounter difficulties when traveling with typical children but try to imagine the worries and stress that are involved in traveling with special needs children. In addition to the emergencies (both medical and non-medical) that are part and parcel of every special needs parent's life, we had to maintain a strict schedule, be organized down to every minute detail, make sure all the medications were packed and a back- up plan for *just-in-case*! As a concrete example, Anthony had to be on eight pills a day for ten days of traveling.

Yet, despite all of these precautions against the what ifs of travel, I urge all of my fellow parents to not give up on your dreams because we did finally make it to Disney World…*Where Dreams Really Do Come True!*

Chapter 10
"The Heart of the Game"
Michael's Diagnosis with ADHD and the Mustangs

As Anthony adjusted to his new life, my family settled into a period of normalcy, peace and happiness, but that soon passed as we turned our attention towards Michael. We knew that Michael was intelligent, but he was having a hard time fitting in socially. He limited his relationships to only one friend at a time. He did not think or behave like a typical 11-year-old, but rather like a stressed-out adult who was emotionally crippled by a heightened sense of anxiety that often culminated in severe migraines. At times, he spoke inappropriately to teachers, family, and friends. He innately understood that he was different from many of his peers. As a parent, I was becoming increasingly concerned because sociability is a vital part of daily life. I came to the realization that something was not quite right, but I was not ready to face that reality. Denial becomes a safe haven for anyone who is not prepared for the truth. I had been blaming Michael's lack of social skills on our family situation, which had caused me to shower his brother Anthony with so much help and support.

So, when Michael announced that that he wanted to play football on the town team, I was absolutely elated. He had been on their wrestling team for a while, but had decided to stop due to the panic attacks caused by the lack of control he felt. Now he wanted to play football. I was well aware that this was a brutally tough contact sport, but if this was what he really wanted to do, then we needed to support him. It definitely helped that his friend Colin also wanted to play football and would be on Michael's team.

During the week, he signed up for the football team; on Saturday afternoon we went for tryouts on the field. All the boys were so excited to be given their football equipment and jerseys. All that was needed now was a crash course on how to properly wear it all! Of course, on the first day of practice, my husband and I went with Michael behind the football shed to check whether he had been able to correctly put on his football gear. It was a good thing that we did because the only piece of equipment he was wearing suitably was his jock strap!

I had informed the coaches that Michael had ADHD and was on prescribed medications. Inwardly, this was an incorrect diagnosis, but I chose not to follow my instinct for once. He wanted to play football so badly that I could not bring myself to end his dream. The first problem that came up was that he would only play the position that was next to Colin. Then, Michael was rigidly determined that everyone on both teams had to follow the rule book to the letter. Michael was adamant: Rules, rules, rules were not meant to be broken! Any deviation from those rules (for example, the wrong call on a play) would send him over the edge. If someone called him a foul name, which happened on several occasions, Michael could not handle it. If the coaches were hard on him, he would shut down for the duration of the practice or the game.

We live in a very competitive sport community, but do the coaches and the parents have to be so obnoxious and aggressive? We were fortunate enough to have very patient coaches that really cared about the children, but a few of the other coaches were absolute fanatics about the outcome of these games. They would teach these young boys to play dirty. "Win, win, win," was the rallying cry and so the score, not sportsmanship, became all that mattered to them.

One fall evening, Michael had a football game on a school night. His pre-game anxiety was even more evident than usual. I could see from the way he was playing defense that something was not sitting well with him. I thought that perhaps the wrist he had broken a few months earlier made him apprehensive about playing such an injury-prone sport. In actuality, that was not the case, but I would have my answer to that puzzle a few years later.

That night, he ran off the field, screaming and yelling that he no longer wanted to play football because it was just too savage a sport for him. I must admit that my first reaction was one of disappointment. Finally, one of my sons was on a sports team just like other boys and it was an awesome feeling while it lasted. I felt as if I were living a normal life for a change. That feeling of being just like every other family had eluded me once again.

That night, I decided to stop being so overprotective because it certainly wasn't benefiting Michael. Children need to be independent and make decisions on their own. They need to learn to engage and connect on their own because there are unintended consequences of our overseeing their every move. Quite simply, we are around them much too much of the time. They need to become more responsible for themselves.

What I have learned as a parent from this experience is that the 24-hour media cycle focuses so much on the dangers and risks of childhood…risks and dangers that I don't remember growing up with when I was a young girl. As a result, we put our children in a protective parental bubble, creating play dates and choosing their range of activities to an excessive level. We rush to save them from any type of hurt, which slows down their ability to develop the life skills needed to navigate any future hardships. We praise them much too often and easily, and, in their need to feel deserving of that lavish praise, they fear disappointing us. We need to let them fail and experience disappointment. They will get over it! What they won't get over is the effects of being overly indulged by parents who want to act as their friends. Let them stand up and fight for what they really value in life on their own. If we treat them as delicate children, they will grow up to be delicate adults. We must prepare them for the real world that awaits them.

It's a tough world out there! Prepare your children for what lies ahead by providing them with a solid foundation that is built upon realistic expectations.

Chapter 11
"My Baby Leaves Home"
Unconditional Love and
a Broken Heart

It was a bitterly cold day in January 2008; despite the bleak landscape, I was in high spirits, driving down a neighborhood street, listening to Journey's "Greatest Hits" CD. (This used to be one of my favorite collections, but now a deep sadness washes over me whenever I hear one of those songs.) The CSE Chairperson from our school district called me on my cell to say that there was something she would like to discuss before our meeting on March 25th. She added that, although she recognized that my husband and I were trying our best with Anthony, it would be in everyone's best interests to consider that he may need 24-hour supervision, with his medications monitored, in a less restrictive environment…in other words, a facility where he would learn and live outside of his home. Her tone was compassionate, but my mom-radar was giving off a warning.

Of course, I immediately responded, "No I can't do that -are you crazy? He's only nine years old! He's still a baby!" She calmly explained, as she must have done for countless mothers before me, that he was a danger to himself and others, and, more ominously, that there really was not all that much of a choice. She went on to point out that the situation would only become more complicated as he got older, that his current situation was not the best placement for him, and that a transition of this kind would become more difficult for Anthony the longer we waited. She asked me to discuss all of these factors with my husband and to have him present at the next IEP meeting. The conversation left me numb, reeling with hurt, anxiety, and fear.

How did she come to this conclusion? I remembered the day, a few weeks earlier, when Anthony's teacher called me to report that he was having an extremely difficult day. He could not be controlled and, as a result, needed to be supervised in their padded room. This is a room where emotionally distraught students are placed so they cannot harm themselves or others. Worried and nervous, I feared that I would not reach my son fast enough; I do not even remember driving to his school. When I arrived, I went straight to his classroom and was met by the principal. We walked to the padded room, with my head spinning, my hands trembling, my heart racing, and my mind not knowing what to expect at this point. The aide opened the door, and there stood my son looking pale, with his eyes glazed over. He had soiled his pants and had thrown up all over himself. I was not only sick to my stomach at what had been done to him, but also incensed by their callousness. I wondered how such treatment could be permitted. Then and there, I made the decision to bring Anthony home with me, never to return to that place. We never looked back.

However, his teacher there was not only passionate about working with special needs children, but also very insightful. Her first priority was always her students, not giving a damn about the backlash. Throughout it all, she gave me positive words of encouragement and excellent advice. She called me "the bulldozer mother" because I simply refused to give up and never stopped trying to help my son. I would demolish any and all obstacles that got in my way. Yet, both she and I knew it was time for him to move on, and that this chapter in his life was over. The next question for us was where to go from here.

When my husband came home from work that night, I told him we needed to discuss something really important. Woodenly, I sat with him, trying to find the right words to tell him what I knew would hurt him so deeply. He asked what was wrong, but the words just would not come out of my mouth. So I repeated the telephone conversation I had had that morning, word for word. He became confused and asked me to repeat what I had said. When my words finally sunk in, he responded in the same way I had done earlier: "No way! He would live where?" In my mind, I knew we needed to do more research with the school district to arrive at the right answers to our questions, but I also felt that our lives were about to change dramatically.

The CSE Chairperson called a few weeks later with the name of a nearby residence for us to visit. My husband and I were desperately trying to keep an open mind. It was a heart-wrenching process, but we knew we had to do what was best for our son. We looked at the day program and residential placement. The children living there ranged from those with severe impairments to those who were higher functioning and included all types of disabilities. The news that the agency had opening for him came all too soon. Since we were in an immediate need and knew the wait list for residential placement was years long, we decided to take it, despite our misgivings.

Although Anthony was no longer at the school, but home in my care, his former teacher continued to encourage me. She was a true blessing. The district decided that he was to continue to receive services at home, but we first needed to stabilize his behaviors and emotions before the academic program could begin. To accomplish this, they sent a behavioral specialist from a private agency nearby. When she first entered my home to assess Anthony, he jumped from a chair onto my dining room table, grabbed the light fixture, screamed, and held a bowl of four hard boiled eggs in his hands, declaring that he was allowed to eat them all - just because he said so! She never blinked an eye, and I knew that another prayer had been answered when she walked through that door. She was intelligent, compassionate, insightful, and wise beyond her years because she knew exactly what my son needed, and that was private placement.

She told me that Anthony fit the profile of most of the children placed where she worked. She advised me to look into it and, if it matched my criteria, to put his name on the waiting list or speak with their social worker. I explained to her that my son had already been approved for the other facility because he needed immediate placement due to the urgency of our family situation. However, I told her I would keep her information for future reference just in case that residence did not work out. My intuition was in overdrive at that point.

Once we had made the decision, I cried every day and every night for weeks and months. Every moment was consumed by my dread of the conversation I needed to have with my son. However, from on high came an inspiration – his idol, Harry Potter! I sat down one night and told Anthony that he was going to Hogwarts School like Harry Potter. He would learn to be a wizard and how to use a wand, and that we would visit him on the weekends. He looked at me trustingly with his big, warm brown eyes and said, "Great, Mommy, I can't wait!" I knew from that moment on that Harry Potter would become our magical transport. Every night, I kept myself busy by ordering furnishings online for his new room: a Harry Potter bedspread, sheets, pillows, owl, wand, lantern, sorting hat, costume, posters, etc. We had a Harry Potter everything! He was so excited and thrilled by this new adventure that I forgot my own pain for a while.

Then my husband and I attended his meeting on March 25th and were told that the placement would occur at the end of June. We left the meeting quietly thinking our own thoughts, but both choked by the heaviness that was in our hearts. I tried to keep my mind filled with positive thoughts every day. One of the most stressful problems was how to tell my traditional Italian parents that their nine-year-old grandson was now going to live away from our home and, even worse, we would not be allowed to visit him for at least 60 days so he could better adjust to the new environment. As Anthony's parents, we were having a hard enough time wrapping our heads around this idea that had been so inconceivable to us just a few months earlier. Imagine what they, the older generation, would think? My head was telling me that I was doing the right thing for my child, but my heart was murmuring an entirely different story.

My husband and I did not speak very much to each other throughout the weeks before our son was to leave home. I feared we had reached a breaking point brought on by the heartbreak we were both undergoing. Each day, the distance between us grew further. I had always known that my husband was able to better detach himself from his emotions. This was a trait that I needed to develop in order to survive this ordeal, and now I knew that my husband would be the only one who could show me the way.

I was very fortunate to have my neighbor Lynn, who made many visits and phone calls to check up on me. She reminded me that Anthony eventually would be coming home for the weekends, and that this was not the worst thing that could happen to a parent. She was most likely remembering that her own son would never come home because he had died in a car accident when he was 18 years old. To revisit that awful day took tremendous courage. Her words made me realize that my situation was not as bad as those of other mothers. I empathized with her pain as never before and cried in her arms.

It came before I knew it: the weekend my baby was to leave home. We had finalized all of the planning. Grandma Frances was to stay over for the weekend to help ease everyone's anguish, especially Michael's. We had bought and labeled all of Anthony's clothing. We had packed all of his Harry Potter accessories and toys. It was time to go. Anthony grabbed my hand and with the other, held onto his baby blanket. Oh my God, was this going to be the absolutely hardest thing I ever had to do in my life?

We arrived at what was going to be his new home. His aunt and godmother were waiting to decorate his room and, most of all, be there for us. We brought in the boxes one by one. Like robots, we made his bed, put his posters up, put Hedwig the owl in the corner of his room, the lantern and wand on his nightstand, and dressed Anthony up like Harry Potter. He looked at us and said, "It's OK... you can go now." I have been reminded on more than one occasion that these children feed off of other's emotions immediately. While trying to appear calm on the outside, inside I was being torn apart. I felt pain I had never felt before in the middle of my chest, my heart was racing, my hands were shaking, and my eyes were swelling up. I had a choking sensation inside my throat, and I could no longer utter a word. I was sad, angry, emotional, tired, guilty, anxious, depressed, nauseous and worried. Can a person safely experience all these emotions at once without exploding?

My husband and I hugged and kissed him, and then it was time to leave him there. As we were walking out the door, we both instinctively turned around...he was still waving goodbye and smiling at us. My heart swelled with pride at his courage. My cousin and my sister-in-law were waiting for us. Once outside, we held each other in an intense group hug, succumbing to our held-in tears and pent-up emotions. Sooner or later, we knew we had to leave the parking lot, but not just yet. Finally, we left, but only because we didn't want our first-born son to see us hysterically crying. He wouldn't understand and might become frightened.

My husband prepared to drive away but had to stop because he was crying with his head on the steering wheel. It was a very intense moment for me because I had never seen his raw emotions so openly in all the years I had known him. He looked at me and asked the question he had kept hidden deep within him for a very long time, "Why my son? He's my namesake." A brief moment later he confessed his worst fear: "If we make it through this, Cathy, we can make it through anything." I echoed his sentiments silently within my heart.

As we drove away, my cousin, who had just left us a few minutes before, called to check on us once more. I tell her truthfully that I didn't know how I was going to make it through this. As always, she replied with words to comfort and encourage me: "You are the strongest woman I know and the best mother in the world. You both are making the ultimate sacrifice of letting him go because you have that unconditional love in your hearts, and you want what's best for him." As you can tell, my cousin is one of my very special soul sisters, that female friend who tends to our inner needs. A soul sister keeps her eye on what really matters, even when we are distracted by life's little annoyances. She never questioned my decision to move Anthony to a specialized residence. She always knows exactly what to say and inspires me to do my very best. She teaches an inclusion (children with developmental delays combined with typically developing children) kindergarten class in Queens, working with children like my son on a daily basis. As a result, she was one of my few friends capable of seeing the full picture.

The drive home was a difficult one. I had such a pain in my chest; it was most definitely my heart breaking. I knew it was now time for me to sit with Michael and explain to this sensitive six-year-old boy that his brother needed to live somewhere else because of his disabilities. He told me something that I already knew… that he didn't think it was fair that God shorted him a brother. To make it hurt less, I taped the most recent photo of him and Anthony to the inside front cover of his first-grade marble notebook. That way, when he missed his brother and was sad in class, he could look at the picture and smile a little.

Finally, I was alone in my bedroom with only my thoughts to keep me company. I knelt on the floor, raised my hands and told God, "I'm releasing my son to you…please keep him safe, warm and wrapped in your arms. Please do this for me, and I shall continue to do your work and to serve those in need the best I can." I put on my pajamas and lay in bed with tears in my eyes, torturing myself with the fear that Anthony thought we had abandoned him, and hoping and praying that no one would hurt him. Even though I was now already second guessing our decision, I knew deep down in my heart that it would have been selfish and irresponsible to have kept him at home, making him more dependent on us. Yet sometimes when we pray for help, and receive the answer we know is right, we still don't like the response.

I knew I was not going to sleep at all that first night. I decided to go to the laundry room where I had left a pair of Anthony's pajamas that he had worn the night before. I made myself a warm cup of tea and slept with his Spiderman pajamas under my cheek so I could touch and smell them. I tormented myself with the idea that children usually leave home at the age of 18 when they are ready for college, not at Anthony's young age. How was I supposed to accept yet another abnormal situation in my life? Would this pain in my chest ever go away? My only comfort was my faith; I had to believe without question that I had made the right decision for my son. Was all this pain part of loving a child unconditionally?

The 60-day waiting period was like a life sentence… unending with no hope in sight. In the meantime, I needed to find the strength to reveal what had happened to my parents, knowing full well what their response would be. My parents were not only upset with our decision, but absolutely furious that we had not included them in this very serious family matter. At first, their outrage blinded them; they accused us of sending Anthony away because it was easier for us, both emotionally and financially. It tore my heart to hear that they would believe that of us. Didn't they realize that I needed them to help me through this crisis? As his mother, I always believed it was my job to take care of him, protect him and raise him, but the situation forced me to send him to live with actual strangers that I had to learn to trust with his well-being and upbringing! I was being torn apart in front of their eyes, but no one, not even my parents, could see my distress.

I was well aware of the close bond between my son Anthony and my mother. From the time he was born, she had watched him so that I could continue to work part-time in human resources for a brokerage firm in downtown Manhattan. However, it was now essential that she both acknowledge and understand that I was his mother. It was a very tough lesson for her. She called me every day like clockwork (sometimes more than once), and if she couldn't reach me at home, she was determined to find me on my cell phone. She informed me of their rights as grandparents and warned me that I could not stop them from seeing him. It was her sorrow and sense of hopelessness that made her speak to me in that way.

At one point, she threatened us with a family court hearing to claim grandparents' rights. She involved my brother and cried on his shoulder, which made him sympathize with them, preventing him from recognizing the sacrifices we had had to make as Anthony's parents. Just when you thought things could not get any worse, somehow, they just do.

May 28, 2008 was one of the most difficult days of my life. My husband and I had a court date for a preliminary proceeding in family court.

I was seeking a court mandated order of protection against my parents and my brother. How had it come to this? When my husband and I finally agreed that Anthony needed outside residential placement and schooling, it was a very private and delicate situation. We knew what we had to do, and really did not wish to discuss the pros and cons with other people, even those closest to us. We knew that everyone would have their own opinions, but, in our fragile state of mind, we could not open the matter up to debate. It was just too painful a subject for us to rehash over and over again, and so we kept our decision secret until we ourselves had come to grips with it. Moreover, since my parents had traditional old-European beliefs, we believed that they would not only be unable to fully understand the complexities of his disabilities, but also that they would be unable to accept that their grandson had become a danger to himself and to others around him. In retrospect, that was a mistaken belief on our part. We had disrespected them by not trusting them.

So, when we brought Anthony to his new home, we decided to tell my parents about it only after the fact. I suppose it was not only my own sense of guilt that led me to think that this was the right move, but also my wish to shield them from the anguish I was going through for as long as possible. I knew that the ties were very close between my parents and my son. As such, I felt that this bond would make it more difficult for them to admit what was right in front of them, making it much easier for them to remain in denial. Why? The truth hurts too much. In other words, this decision to send Anthony to another residence was tantamount to admitting that we had failed him as a family. That was a tremendous burden to have lain upon their shoulders; I knew because I was falling down from the weight of it all.

However, the choice we had made not to keep my parents informed about Anthony's placement had serious repercussions. My parents and brother felt hurt at being left out of this decision and made those feelings clear in every conversation we had with one another. These family discussions continued for a few months, never letting up and only worsening as time went by. Fueled by anxiety and with my emotions running wild, I filed for court orders of protection against my parents and brother. A word of advice: never allow your emotions to take control of your actions. While it is true that we all have the free will to make a choice, it is also true that you cannot choose the consequences of that choice. As a result of my choice, summonses were served against my parents and brother, accompanied by manipulative lawyers, unnecessary legal fees, ugly court appearances, and a family torn apart by their deep and abiding love for this one child.

The day arrived for the preliminary hearing, and I was sick to my stomach. I had a pounding headache brought on by anticipation of the coming confrontation at the courthouse. The family gathered in the waiting area along with our lawyers. We sat facing each other on opposite sides of the room. It was surreal. We were finally called into the courtroom. The judge had already reviewed the case file along with the five-inch stack of Anthony's records. She peered down at all of us and pointed out that in her personal observation and opinion, we did not belong there because we did not fit the typical profile of the petitioners present in her courtroom. She then instructed us to discuss the issues outside the courtroom and come to an agreement together as a family with our lawyers present. Once we had finished, we were to come back to schedule a court date. Before we left, she asked my parents to look at me and ask themselves if I appeared to be calm, unconcerned, and not distraught over what was happening to my child and my family. In fact, I had been hiding behind my husband, holding back my tears, with fluttering hand movements, trying to control my oncoming panic attack.

The judge was wise because just by looking at us, she knew that we would come to an agreement regarding visitation rights for my parents. I could never have kept either of my children away from them. Not only had they always been loving parents to me, but it would have been an injustice on my part to try to break them apart. Ultimately, the judge showed us that it would have been very selfish for my husband and me to take that away from them. If we had not stepped into her courtroom that day, I believe my relationship with my parents and brother would have been irreparably damaged. I took a drastic step that I knew had to be taken to end a situation that was endangering my family unit. Sometimes we need to confront our fears head-on in order to abolish them altogether.

Over time, our family relationship was mended. The path was not an easy one, and there were many missteps along the way. However, we all worked at it because we knew that our efforts would eventually bring us closer together, with a better understanding as to the true meaning of family. My son Anthony needed us to be together as a family, now more than ever before.

In the meantime, my husband and I grappled with our own uncertainties, brought on by criticism from outsiders. We realized that only time would tell what improvements and setbacks were ahead for our child, but we had made the decision to take that chance for his future. We feared that we had cast him off into an unknown abyss, but our only chance of survival was to hope against hope that the choice we had made would give our son a life of independence, with no one but himself to rely on for his daily needs. This is the life that parents of typically developing children take for granted; it is so difficult for them to truly appreciate how blessed they are to have a child that is able to go to school by bus without supervision, eat with utensils, bathe alone, do homework, have friends, play sports, communicate and express their emotions appropriately, with no medications required to function in the real world. In other words, I mean all of the everyday activities that most of the children like Anthony need to be taught consistently and routinely every day, with support from skilled professionals and often harried parents.

Even my best friend was upset and disappointed with me when I chose to place Anthony away from my home, refusing to allow me to discuss my feelings with her as well as the reasons why we had done what we had done. I needed a friend to just listen to my pain, but helping me find a way to survive during this darkest period of my life was the furthest thing from her mind. Instead, she asked if she could keep him and raise him, which felt like a slap in the face. Yet, I loved her for her offer because I knew that her heart was as broken as mine and this way her way of coping. It was simply her maternal instincts coming out. She never intended to hurt me, but clutched at the chance to raise my child since she was unable to have children of her own.

To this day, it's still troubles me that most of the people I know and love could not understand that it was love that drove us to make this ultimate sacrifice and decision. Perhaps this was because it was the love that surpasses understanding, but the simple truth was that we did not have much of a choice. We had to be realistic; the reality was that although he appeared to be absolutely perfect on the outside, only we, his parents, knew firsthand the debilitating disabilities that plagued his inner soul. The fact that his symptoms were not outwardly evident made it extremely difficult for others to agree with what they felt was an extreme measure on our part. They never realized that the situation had finally reached a point where his disabilities were becoming increasingly difficult for us to manage on our own. There were just too many doctors, too many decisions to be made, too many specialists to see, too many schools, evaluations, and IEP meetings…and Anthony was not getting any better!

I always say that family, friends and outsiders live the commercial, while my husband and I live the movie. They would spend holidays and a few hours with you and then - not only did they judge you, but they also believed that they had the antidote for all of your problems. Such well-meaning people should be gently reminded that children are not like shoes; if they don't quite fit, or are damaged, you cannot return your son or daughter for new ones, or, better yet, ask for a refund! These children certainly did not expect to be born like this, nor did their parents. It just is what it is, but it will become what we choose to make of it. I knew that my son did not want to suffer with the mind with which he was born. I had to let go in order to help him!

Why were so many of my family and friends unable to see our despair at that time? I thought I would have a nervous breakdown from trying to save my family and my marriage. The divorce rate of parents of special needs children is 80% on average. I was well aware of that statistic, having seen it firsthand with other couples in our same situation. All of us were feeling miserable with only the slimmest of hopes to sustain us, which was that there had to be better days ahead.

In less than a year, Anthony left his first residence, which had been chosen because it was the only placement available at that time. The district felt, as did we, that he needed an immediate placement because he was in danger of harming himself and others. We had felt that it was going to be just a temporary home for him because much of the population consisted of lower functioning children. That being the case, there was a serious lack of academics and technology in the school, two areas that Anthony required to improve his future lifestyle.

During this period, I had stayed in touch with the behavior specialist at the private school and had kept her abreast of my concerns with the original placement. She made a private appointment for us to look at the school and residential placement. I did this without the requisite permission from the school district because I didn't want to have to wait for them to go through the usual administrative and political machinations that would give me permission to obtain this appointment. I was tired of jumping through hoops, listening and waiting for no one. After our visit, I informed the CSE Chairperson that I judged this agency to be the best place for my son and that they had a bed open and waiting for him. I knew from experience to explain the legitimate reasons why my husband and I felt he needed to be moved. In a few weeks, the final move took place. We packed everything from that first residence and moved Anthony to the place that my intuition told me would be right for him and for us.

At the conclusion of this chapter, which I wrote with great difficulty and an outpouring of tears at the memory of it all, I feel that it is my duty to remind those that are not walking in another person's shoes not to judge, comment, or even qualify themselves to understand someone else's decisions. If you haven't actually lived through a situation, whatever it may be, please realize that you have no right to second guess what is being done. You are entitled to your opinion, but sometimes careless words have a negative impact... so my sincere advice is to keep them to yourself. Your inner thoughts really do not need to be expressed, and they may likely hurt the other person beyond measure as well as your relationship with them. Think before you speak and check your own misgivings at the door; thoughtless words always hurt, are never forgotten, and continue to have profound repercussions on those you love!

Chapter 12
"911"
Is Our Baby Going to be Alright?

It was October 29, 2007; one of those breathtakingly beautiful days that only occur in the fall. The air was crisp, the sun bright and the leaves had turned to those amazing hues of copper, purple, and bronze. It was the christening day of my cousin's newborn son...a day of hope and new beginnings. My boys were excitedly looking forward to spending time with their cousins. We were all so happy, never imagining the night to come.

As my husband was parking in front of the restaurant, I heard Anthony shout hello to his grandparents. Both of the boys could not run out of the car fast enough for some hugs and kisses. We climbed the stairway to the main dining hall and, as we passed the kitchen, the smell of fresh bread and Italian food was mouthwatering. Michael looked up at me with his chubby cheeks and twinkling eyes to solemnly announce, "Mommy I want 'pasghetti' with lots of sauce and cheese."

We sat at the table with my parents, my brothers, their wives, and my four gorgeous nieces. My sons always enjoyed sitting in the middle of their girl cousins because they received so much love and attention from them. It was so nice to have everyone sitting at the table, eating delicious food and drinking Italian wine, while talking to each other a mile a minute! In the meantime, Anthony and Michael were having their own fun dancing and playing with their cousins. The best part was that we were all soaking in some quality family time for a change.

Shortly after the abundant meal, we were served espresso, cappuccino, fresh fruits, and a selection of Italian and Greek cookies. After all, what's a European celebration without the all-important Venetian Hour? There was a short moment during dessert when my son Anthony was taking a personal tour of the tables. Of course, a boy with the face of an angel was able to cajole the guests into giving him fresh watermelon from their tables. He returned to me licking his lips, with sticky fingers and watermelon seeds stuck to his face.

Grandma Angela took him to the bathroom to wash away the mess. "Grandma my tummy hurts." A short hour later, his eyes glazed over and his body suddenly appeared weary and overly fatigued. We quickly said our good-byes and left for home.

When we arrived home, Anthony had fallen into a deep sleep, so my husband placed him on the couch in the den and I brought Michael to his bed. I had undressed, but decided to catch up on some reading in the den in order to watch Anthony, Jr. sleep.

After two hours, it was time to wake him for his 8:00 pm seizure medications. I remember thinking to myself that I hated to disturb him. Before I had the opportunity to do so, I saw that his body was shaking violently, his eyes were rolling, and drool was oozing out of his mouth. I screamed for my husband, "Anthony's having a grand mal seizure!" My husband became white as a ghost, frozen in fear at the unfamiliar sight. My cries awakened Michael from his deep sleep. That was when my mind and body went into overdrive, rushing to place Anthony on his side and making sure that he would not bite his tongue. I silently prayed that he would be alright.

In the meantime, my husband's reflexes also kicked in. He called 911 and the emergency team was inside our home in a matter of minutes. Although his seizure lasted three to four minutes, the horror of it felt like an eternity; time stood still, and all of the activity passed before me in slow motion. It was just like one of those terrible dreams when you just want to wake up so that the nightmare could end.

When the seizures finally stopped, I had to jumpstart my husband back into reality. It was also critical that I comfort Michael because the look of fear and anxiety on his face was painfully obvious. At one point, I was actually afraid that the paramedics would also have to resuscitate my husband.

Knowing that Anthony would become frightened if he woke up in the middle of an ambulance trip, we decided to use a police escort while driving to the hospital in our own car. I wrapped him in a blanket and carried him in my arms just like I had done when he was a baby. I kept checking to see if he was breathing. On the way, I called my parents to meet us at the hospital to take Michael safely home with them.

In the emergency room, the staff ran blood tests to check his levels of medications. The emergency room doctor asked if he had eaten anything out of the ordinary that could have caused the seizures. I knew in the pit of my stomach that the likely catalyst to his grand mal seizure was the natural sugars in all the watermelon slices he had eaten at the party. Although I had no idea that a high amount of sugar could cause seizures, the guilt I felt as his mother flooded my senses like a strong and bitter pill. Even after all these years, I have never forgotten the feeling.

That night my husband and I brought Anthony home and he slept in our bed. We were both so shaken up that neither one of us slept. The next day we brought Anthony to the neurologist that had first diagnosed him with epilepsy and ADHD at the age of three. We waited patiently to be called, expecting the usual ninety-minute wait. However, since it was an emergency visit, we did not have to wait that long. As we anxiously sat in front of him, the doctor reviewed the blood level test results from the night before.

After what seemed like an hour, he looked directly at me, and in an arrogant, loud, obnoxious tone, snarled, "How does it feel to be responsible for your son's first grand mal seizure?" My husband was astounded: "Excuse me!" The doctor shortly responded, "You heard me." I was not surprised. Although this doctor had come highly recommended by my pediatrician, my intuition made me wary of him from the moment we first met. He struck me as a cold person with no empathy at all for his patients - not a good trait in a pediatric neurologist that had to work with scared young children and their worried families.

I took a deep breath, looked him in the face and said the words that had been on my mind all of those years: "Just because you have that degree on the wall does not give you permission to speak to a mother like that! A good doctor has compassion and understanding for his patients." Knowing my temperament, my husband stood between the almighty doctor and me. All my pent-up emotions were evident on my face. Since my son was sitting there, I controlled myself with the assurance that I would get even with this doctor by working to make sure that I and no other parent would have to undergo his abuse again. True to my word, as I walked out of his office, I asked for my son's file and told the nurses that Anthony would no longer be a patient there. I then proceeded to report his unprofessionalism to the New York State Medical Board.

Yet, that doctor's accusation had cut me deeply; the hurt, worry and pain were almost unbearable. I knew I had to put his sneering words behind me in order to give Anthony the help he needed. I prayed for the strength to forget and go forward.

I found that strength in the morning. I made a call to my trusted pediatrician who, after hearing about my experience, gave me the name of a new neurologist. I met with her the next day and she changed his meds, which has made all the difference for Anthony. She continues to monitor him to this day with skill, patience, and best of all, understanding.

Chapter 13
"The Stalking of Dr. Z"
Road Trip With My BFF

So, my BFF's name is Patty; she and her husband are Michael's godparents. She was one of the first people to hold both my children when they were born. She has never left my side, has always had my back and, most importantly, is forever the friend that has always been just a phone call away, no matter what. My nickname for her is "Pyramid of Information" since she is so intelligent and informative. She can come up with a fool-proof plan or solution to any dilemma in a matter of minutes (and sometimes seconds!)

We don't have to communicate with one another on a daily basis, but when we do touch base, we just pick up where we left off as if no time had passed. You know who I mean…*that* friend, the one who comes over in her pajamas, bunny slippers and robe to knock on your front door to make sure all is well. She was the one that went with me to the emergency room at midnight on the Sunday when my son dislocated his elbow. Even then, she eased my stress by making me laugh at the poor patient in the next bed who had glued her eyes shut with Crazy Glue. (She had mistakenly used it in the dark instead of her prescription eye drops.)

When I first thought there was something not quite right with my son Anthony, she never once questioned my apprehension. So many others pooh-poohed my mounting fear, but not her; she believed in my intuition. Like a second mother, Patty had recognized the signs for herself. Anthony was speech-delayed, his eyes became trance-like at times, and he occasionally drooled. He could never sit still, had no memory recall, had a hard time socializing with children his age, was defiant with his teachers, and had extreme separation anxiety.

Being the person that she is, Patty never left my side even while she was going through the difficulty of trying to conceive a child of her own. Some women are born to be mothers and she was definitely one of them. Unfortunately, without rhyme or reason, it just did not happen for her. Why is it that some women that should not have children are able to conceive, and some of the most deserving women cannot? I guess you could say some questions can never be answered. What happened to my dear friend was another example of one of life's awful mysteries.

As my best friend and confidante, Patty knew that I had been struggling with Anthony's development issues for quite some time. She reminded me about the session Anthony had had a few years earlier with Dr. Z, a prominent child psychiatrist. My son had shown great improvements after Dr. Z's evaluation and change in medications. She suggested it was time to take Anthony for a follow-up visit.

I called his phone number, only to learn that Dr. Z had relocated to another university upstate. I knew he was very much in demand, but I was a mom on a mission, desperate to make an appointment with him. I left numerous messages at his office. I refused to give up. Finally, he returned my call to explain that he was teaching students during the day. If I wanted to see him, it would have to be at the university after 3:00 pm. He also informed me that the fee would be $300 per visit, with no insurance accepted. Dr. Z also mentioned that he knew that if he did not meet with me, I would continue calling him until he did. He was most definitely correct! His expertise in psychiatry was clearly evident in his assessment of my utter determination.

My next step was to give Patty the good news. I told her the appointment details and, as usual, she was ready to go that day! Her exact words were, "Confirm the appointment and don't waste any time. We need to do this now!"

On July 31, 2007, Patty came to pick us up and we were on our way. She even made the ride there seem like a breeze. We made that same trip at least four times. She never complained about the traffic, never wanted any money for gas, and silently listened to my endless concerns and worries. I will always remember how, before one of the visits, Anthony had a yen for McDonald's just as we had arrived at the psychiatrist's office. Instead of becoming exasperated, she looked at him with assurance and said, "I will find you one." However, according to the security guard at the university, there was only one McDonalds in the area, which was located all the way on the other side of town with no easy access to parking.

Patty was up for the challenge; she made a U-turn out of the university parking lot and declared, "We have half an hour…I will find it." I never doubted her word for a minute. In two blinks of an eye, Anthony had his Happy Meal, Aunty Patty got a huge kiss and hug, and we were on our way back to the office. I am convinced that she hides her Superwoman cape under her clothes.

On the last and fourth visit, we were to learn the diagnosis, be prescribed a change of medications, as well as a specific behavioral and daily living plan that was to be submitted to the school district. I always knew in my heart of hearts that there was a missing piece to my son. We were about to finally discover what that missing piece was.

I will never forget that last visit. We entered Dr. Z's office; Anthony was playing with blocks on the floor, while Patty and I sat across from him. Dr. Z handed me the plan of action but was having a very difficult time reviewing the diagnosis with me. I kindly looked at him and said, "Dr. Z, we haven't come all this way not to know. Please tell me your analysis of Anthony without any more hesitation. I just can't take it." He replied with some relief, "You are a no-nonsense kind of mother. I usually need to use kid gloves when speaking to parents in situations like these, but not with you."

He solemnly continued with the words I long dreaded yet expected to hear: "My diagnosis is that your son has Pervasive Developmental Disorder; it falls within the Autism Spectrum." Releasing the breath I had been holding for several years now, I answered him: "OK, at least now I know what I'm dealing with." I remembered all those evaluations that had been carried out in the years since Anthony was three years old, not one of them yielding the full truth. The wording was always tempered with "possibly" …or "maybe."

I turned towards my friend who was sobbing uncontrollably. She was always known as the ice princess. She rarely cries, but when she does, she cannot stop. She apologized for her outburst, saying, "I was supposed to be here to support you. My heart is breaking for you." In the next breath, she demanded to know why I wasn't crying – me, who cries at Hallmark commercials! I felt a strange sense of calm mixed with relief, a feeling I had not experienced since I first heard my inner voice telling me that something was amiss with my oldest child. I felt vindicated, but more importantly, now I knew I had a concrete plan of action to follow. As I explained to my sobbing friend, "It's better to know than not to know. Now I can start to do what I have to do." And that is exactly what I did.

Chapter 14
"The Greatest Little Surprise"
My Shadow's Name is Jake

Who doesn't want a puppy for Christmas? My husband! Why? Well, dear reader, read on…

Whenever the subject of a family dog came up (and in our house, that question was raised on a regular basis), his response invariably was, "They are a lot of work, money, responsibility - and if something happens to the dog, it's heartbreaking for everyone. Besides, I know that I'm going to end up walking the dog and picking up after him." My stubbornly optimistic reply: "If you love me and the kids, you would let us have a puppy!" I was not about to give up!

It was Christmas of 2006 when I first asked Santa for a puppy for Christmas and my husband said we needed to discuss it further. So that's exactly what we did. I went online and looked up some breeds. My perfect dog would not be too big, with a sweet temperament, intelligent, not hyper or a yapper, and, most important of all, had to be good with children. Why? Excluding the intelligence trait, the description of my perfect pet was designed to be the exact opposite of my children. If the puppy turned out to be anything like my children, I could see that my future fashion accessory would not be straight out of *Vogue*, but instead the very special white jacket. You know the one I mean… one size fits all, with the straps that tie your arms around you! A mischievous puppy that enjoyed barking all day and night would turn my home into the next "Amityville Horror House," if you know what I mean!

Despite my hidden fears, I was determined to forge ahead with my plan to bring a puppy into our lives. We started out on our quest to find the perfect pup, but there were so many stores and so little time! Every one of them boasted a full collection of small, adorable, playful, pooping and peeing puppies. Every weekend, we visit several pet stores with my three "boys" in tow, including my husband as part of the trio. (You women know what I'm talking about.) We would pick out a few puppies, and an employee would bring them out, one at a time, into the meet and greet puppy play area. However, the trek that had begun as a fun family activity soon became tiresome as weeks turned into months.

Finally, in the fall of 2007 my husband asked (with a bit of impatience), "What exactly are you looking for in a puppy?" I patiently explained the obvious to him by pointing out that no matter how many precious puppies we met, none of them had been the right dog for us. As he stared at me further with a puzzled look on his face, I informed him that we would not be continuing our search. If it was meant for us to have a puppy, he would find us. I heard skepticism in his next question: "How would he find us?" I spelled it out for him: "Just like everything else. The big man upstairs knows what we want, and if this special puppy exists, our paths will meet." Of course, his just-like-a-man response was, "OK, I get it - you're having a moment of clarity."

Christmas 2007 came and went, and still no puppy appeared. Three months passed and we were now in April. It was a beautiful spring day and I decided to go buy cold cuts at my favorite deli. As I was ordering, I ran into Ellen who worked for the school district in our area. She informed me that she was taking some time off to do something that had been her dream for many years. Then, she pulled out a pocket-size photo album of her new breed of puppies, totaling eight in all. I could not believe how beautiful they were! Six females and two males, each a blend of the King Charles Cavalier and French Poodle breeds, looked up at me appealingly from the photos. The one that captured my heart had curly beige hair with spots of brown, accentuated by spots of white on his head and paws. With my heart in my mouth, I asked if he belonged to anyone yet. I was thrilled when she replied, "No, and isn't it funny that you picked the one male I have left?"

I could barely contain my excitement and immediately called my husband from the store to announce that I had found the perfect puppy. "In actuality, Anthony, like I told you, he found us. I'm taking the boys to see him tonight and leave a deposit." He persisted, "How do you know he's the one?" I pronounced with finality, "I just do." I took down her personal information and told her we would be at her home around 6:00 pm that night.

The day could not have passed any slower. As soon as the boys came home from school, I told them my happy news. Now the boys were just as impatient as I was, so around 5:30 pm we headed to Ellen's home with our hopes and heads both held high. We rang the bell and finally Ellen answered the door. She told us that the puppies were upstairs being fed by their mom. We followed Ellen upstairs in quiet (at least for us) anticipation. In the room we found eight precious "Cavapoo" puppies resting in a feeding bed with their mom. What a thrill it was for us! No sooner did I sit on the floor, when one of the puppies left his mother and began circling around my feet. He had beautiful brown eyes, a curly tail, and white spots on his paws and head. It was the puppy from the picture! I knew right then and there that he was meant to be our long-awaited pet. He was so playful and sweet. Of course, I just wanted to take him home right then and there, but I knew that he needed to stay with his mom for a few more weeks.

Now that we had finally found him, it was time to shop for the newest member of our family. We made a beeline for Petco, buying him a bed, brush, puppy food, snacks, carrying case, harness and a leash. Of course, like most women, I hid the bill from my husband.

The prescribed four long weeks had passed, and it was time for us to pick him up. He had had his first round of shots and was healthy enough to leave the litter. My husband and I brought a baby blanket to keep him warm. It reminded me of those special, never-to-be-forgotten days when we carried each of our newborn sons home. I wrapped him in the baby blanket and he had his eyes closed. He was absolutely perfect! I felt joy swelling up within me.

That night, we had a family discussion on names and chose Jake, which means both "healer" and "most satisfactory." That was exactly what my family needed at that time. My son Anthony Jr. was to leave our home that summer to live in his school residence, and along came Jake in the spring of that same year. My family desperately needed some type of diversion to take our minds off of the pending move, and Jake was it. When I cried about the upcoming separation from my child, Jake lay consolingly at my feet, barking only when necessary. When the sadness bubbled up deep within my soul, he would kiss my hands and played patiently with my children. Jake followed me closer than my shadow, slept next to me on my bedroom floor, and cuddled next to me as I read a book or watched television. He needed me and I needed him. He saved my life! He's my joy and gift from Heaven, bringing me from one unconditional love to the next.

Chapter 15
"The Man in the Electric Blue Dodge Ram Truck with Bright Silver Rims"
Child Protective Services

Wow how time flies! It was October 2006 and Michael had been attending kindergarten for the past month at our local elementary school. Anthony Jr. was attending the local school for special needs children.

Anthony's bus arrived at 8:45 am, which was no guarantee that he would easily cooperate and board it. What do I mean by this? Well, he might throw down his knapsack, curse, kick, scream, yell, punch, bite, maybe take off his clothes or, worst case scenario, decide to run off as soon as he saw his bus coming. This would occur on a daily basis, meaning that every day I would awaken with my heart racing and my anxiety soaring through the roof because I never knew what to expect from Anthony's erratic moods and behavior. If there were no incidents during the morning pick-up, then I would await the dreaded phone calls from school during the day.

In harsh contrast, his brother Michael had excitedly put on his Spiderman knapsack, grabbed his lunchbox, and eagerly waited in the hallway for his bus. Considering all the chaos that goes on in our home, it's only natural that he would be happy to have a change of scenery. When his bus arrived, he grabbed my hand, kissed my cheek and ever so sweetly told me to be safe and have a nice day.

Anthony, on the other hand, found transitioning from home to school very difficult, which meant that the bus ride to and from school was pure misery for all concerned. The one and only saving grace was that the bus driver and matron demonstrated tremendous patience, compassion and care towards every child on that bus. We knew that they did not perform their job just for a paycheck. They loved what they did; it showed on their faces.

For parents of special needs children who have siblings, there is a pervasive feeling of guilt. We have to devote so much time and attention to the child with severe disabilities, constantly working with them, filling out forms, taking them to specialists and therapists, and remaining vigilant to their wants and requirements. In my case, I regretted that I never had the time to just sit with Michael and give him the one-on-one attention that he needed to learn the alphabet, numbers, reading, etc. As a result, he struggled with academics. Yet, although he often lived in Anthony's shadow, he has become very independent and quite mature because he had to learn to make it on his own.

Finally, after what seemed like forever, both my children were on their way to school. I turned my attention to my typical weekday regimen of washing breakfast dishes, refilling the usual prescriptions for my son, doing laundry, running errands, paying bills and preparing dinner. Since it was such a beautiful crisp autumn day, I wanted to finish as much I could so that when they arrived home, we could have fun outside. The afternoon started as planned. We had been playing a great game of whiffle ball for at least an hour. Anthony displayed amazing strength when he hit that ball. It cleared houses upon houses. As he forcefully hit one of my pitches, I raced to retrieve the ball that had shot clear across the street. As I was turning to run back with it, I saw an electric blue Dodge Ram truck with bright silver rims pull up in front of our house.

A gentleman emerged from the truck, clipboard in hand. As quick as a mother hen, I began running hurriedly towards my children when I heard him ask, "Which one of you is Anthony Jr.?" I knew to ask for some identification, and then learned he was with Child Protective Services. He was there because the agency had received a formal complaint of abuse from the school. He requested that we go into my home to prevent the neighbors from hearing our discussion. I asserted that I had nothing to hide but went inside at his insistence. Once inside, he informed me that an aide in Anthony's classroom had noticed a black and blue mark on his leg and reported it to the school. He turned towards Anthony and asked my son to show him the bruise; he inspected it with microscopic intensity. Then he questioned and spoke to both my children separately.

Afterwards, he informed me that my husband could be removed from the home if the investigation confirmed that the bruise was caused by abuse. I tried to explain that my son Anthony had attempted to jump from one captain bed to the other while reaching for the ceiling fan. He fell down as my husband tried to catch him, banging his leg hard on the headboard as he tumbled onto his bed. My defenses were up:

"Do you have any idea what it is like to raise a special needs child?"

He stared directly at me and responded,

"I'm not the one beating my kids."

I could not believe what I was hearing.

"You think we're beating our children?"

His tone of voice grew very loud and confrontational.

"Just because he's disabled doesn't mean you have the right to beat him!"

I was absolutely flabbergasted; my insides churned in disbelief, followed by a deep sense of rage and nausea at what I had just heard.

As little as he was, Michael had the sense to seek out my neighbor Lynn who lived around the corner. He described a bad man talking to Mommy and that he said he wanted to take Daddy away. She immediately rushed into my home to question his authority and the reason for his visit. Outraged by his accusations, she defended me, saying that I was "a very attentive, loving, and caring mother that would never raise her hands to her children." She went on to say that my boys were very active, often injuring themselves as a result. She then advised him that he was in the wrong house and needed to go where he was really needed. He coolly explained that his experience had taught him that children were abused behind closed doors, often in the best neighborhoods. She looked back at him just as coolly and replied,

"Not here…not in this house! She's a woman of faith!"

He retorted,

"Even women of faith are capable of beating their children!"

I escorted him to the door with tears in my eyes, my stomach tied up in a bundle of nerves, and my head pounding from a massive migraine. Michael kept asking if the bad man was coming back for his dad, or his brother, or possibly him. I hugged and kissed him on his forehead and told him not to worry.

In the coming weeks, this same inspector came to question my children at their schools. Phone calls and letters from Child Protective Services arrived almost daily. Every time I heard from them, I became sick to my stomach. I had to communicate with a social worker each and every day during the investigation. It was a horrendous, despicable, and frightening ordeal. Then, after three months of humiliation, stress, and prying investigations, all charges were dropped. No apologies were ever given.

For the longest time afterwards, I would replay the visit from the man in the electric blue Dodge Ram truck with bright silver rims in my head. I knew deep down inside he was only doing his job, but I still stung from the accusations. The memory of it all made me keep questioning our parenting skills, allowing Anthony to go "where the wild things are" every once in a while. Each time I came to the same conclusion. As parents, we were trying our best with what God gave us, but it was simply impossible to be everywhere for everyone all the time. So, we needed to forgive him and ourselves. It was essential to our happiness as a family to put this entire experience behind us once and for all. Wallowing in doubt and self- pity wasn't getting us anywhere. We had to rely on the hope that future days would be better.

Chapter 16
"The Dreaded Phone Call - One of Many"
I'm So Sorry, Mr. Officer

It had been a couple of nights of interrupted sleep, or no sleep at all. Just a few days before, we had received a court summons taken out by a supposedly close friend of mine, who was suing us for an incident that occurred in our home while she was babysitting our two children, one of whom is disabled. As I tossed and turned, I thought about what else I would have to deal with in the future. You know that saying *my plate is full?* Well, my plate is not a plate, but a very large platter!

Unlike his brother Michael, Anthony Jr. was the little boy we could never get to board the school bus in the morning without causing a problem. His tantrums had become our morning routine. I knew that I loved him beyond words, but what I didn't know was how to help him.

I know that I have mentioned before that I was extremely grateful for his matron and bus driver who were my angels in disguise. These ladies had the patience and compassion that are rarely seen with such consistency on this earth. The love and acceptance they showered on those children was totally without boundaries. Even though I knew Anthony could not help being the way that he was, I must admit that there were days when I just did not want to be the mother of that kid who could not control himself or behave properly. Whenever those thoughts flashed into my brain, the accompanying guilt would inevitably find its way in as well.

During this time, I had become accustomed to receiving a phone call from the school every day (sometimes twice) about Anthony's inappropriate behaviors at school. It was a few minutes past noon on March 2, 2005 when the phone rang. I had just sat down to fold some laundry so I looked at my caller id and saw that it was the school. Although I had come to expect these daily calls, my heart began racing with fear, and my mind became anxious. It was the principal from Anthony's school, informing me that my son had had a major meltdown, but that he could not give me details over the phone. In a concerned voice, he instructed me to be there within 15 minutes or they would have to take him by ambulance to be admitted to the hospital. I questioned if Anthony was seriously hurt, but his brief response was that we would talk when I arrived at the school.

In a state of panic, I jumped into my car and took off, fully aware that I only had a few minutes to get to that school before the ambulance would be there to take my baby away. All I kept repeating to myself was to take deep breaths…deep breaths and I would arrive safely and on time. The drive there felt like forever. I prayed as I drove onto the parkway, not realizing I was driving at least 70 miles an hour. As I passed Exit 24, I saw flashing lights behind my car. All I could think of was getting to Exit 25 where my son was waiting for me.

Ignoring the consequences, I had made up my mind: I was not going to pull over. I watched the police car in my rear-view mirror as it closely followed me off the exit and to the front of the school. As I rushed out of my car, the officer approached me and asked why I was speeding and told me to show him my license and registration. I resolutely answered, "Officer, my son goes to this school. You can do what you have to do, but I'm going into the building right now because my son is not well. This is an emergency!" As I turned to dash up the stairs, I handed him my wallet and told him to write whatever tickets he felt were necessary. I then promised that I would come out after I saw my son.

My hands were sweaty; I thought my heart was going to come out of my chest as I ran to his classroom. There, I found Anthony lying in a fetal position on the floor in a corner of the room. He had trashed the entire classroom, flipping over the desks, ripping schoolwork off the walls, and finally passing out from the intensity of his rage. He had become so out of control that he had to be isolated away from the other students while the staff monitored his actions through the door. I picked him up off the floor and saw that his pants were soiled. He was sleeping peacefully. Could this be the same child that had so violently wrecked his classroom? I walked down the hallway carrying him in my arms like a baby and stepped out through the front door.

The officer was waiting by my car; he looked at my face and didn't say a word. I put Anthony in his booster seat and went over to the officer. In a sympathetic voice, he observed, "You look like you're having a very difficult day." I began to cry and hyperventilate. I asked him to please quickly write up my tickets so I could leave. He revealed that his nephew was autistic, and that he knew what type of school it was when he pulled up in front. He ended by telling me that I had a clean driving record, gave me a verbal warning, and urged me to drive carefully so that I would bring my child home safely. I was very fortunate that the officer was understanding and decent. This terrible day could have ended up very differently if had decided to place me in handcuffs for not pulling over; I could have very well been arrested for ignoring his directions. Even worse, my reckless driving may have injured not only myself, but others. This was a blessing in disguise, confirming my belief in the existence of guardian angels that unexpectedly appear to save us from ourselves.

As I tried to find out what was at the bottom of Anthony's outburst, I remembered that his neurologist had put him on the ADHD medication Adderall, which had been giving him bad headaches that were making him very irritable. Since this medication had received some negative reviews, I was reluctant about putting him on it. Unfortunately, I did not listen to my inner voice and trusted the neurologist instead. This was a major life lesson: doctors and specialists are not always right!

As parents and guardians, we must remind doctors of the fact that we are with our children all day, every day. Therefore, we know them better than anyone else. The fact is that most physicians and specialists come in contact with our children for less than an hour every month or every three months, yet they believe they know what's best for them. From my perspective, this does not make sense. One of the most important roles we have as parents is to inform the professionals about our children to help them see the full picture. At times, we will need to strongly express our disagreement with the doctor, no matter how renowned he or she is, and in doing so, you will discover that your opinion will not only be heard, but valued.

Chapter 17
"Where do I Belong?"
Anthony Jr. is Permanently Removed
From Kindergarten

It is August 12, 2003, a day I was not looking forward to: my district meeting for Anthony Jr.'s transition from pre-school to kindergarten. At the time, he was labeled "Other Health Impaired." Anthony's godmother, an experienced special education teacher, decided to accompany me to this meeting because my emotions were on overdrive. At the meeting, it was decided that he would be placed in another elementary school that housed a self-contained kindergarten.

His kindergarten teacher there had a heart of gold and was especially dedicated to my son. As a skilled, compassionate teacher, she knew that his transition into kindergarten was going to be challenging. He was having trouble recognizing letters and numbers, struggling to pay attention, having mild seizures, and battling with himself and others to fit into his new surroundings. She would take time to sit with him every day in order to help and observe him. It was easy to see that a special relationship was developing between them. However, the administrative staff was not experienced or qualified enough to even have a child like Anthony in the building. I received one phone call after the next, which only heightened my sense of uneasiness with the situation.

I just had this intense, recurring feeling that they did not want my son in that school. The principal appeared to have a heart made of stone. For example, on one occasion my son called him a liar; Anthony's reason for doing so was that he had been provoked by the principal's dishonesty, but as a punishment, Anthony was sent straight to the principal's office. I later discovered that his explanation was not that far off from the truth. I saw how my son was trying to adapt and do what was expected of him. Unfortunately, his efforts failed; I was so frustrated and upset and it broke my heart (not the first, or the last, of many such heartbreaks.)

I began to understand why he fought so hard not to get on the "big boy" bus in the morning. Every day it was a different story. One day, in order to escape, he ran around the corner, past my neighbor's home. I had no choice but to let the bus leave without him because Anthony was nowhere in sight. He could run like the wind; it made him feel both free and in control at the same time. My neighbor reacted without hesitation, jumping into his car to begin searching for my son. Thank God for my neighbors! He found him several blocks away. After placing him safely in the car, he asked what was wrong. Anthony told him, "I don't belong in that school." He came home in tears. I decided it would be best if he stayed home, considering the difficult morning. I also feared what would happen at school that day.

In February 2004, I felt that it was important to discuss the situation privately with my district's special education director. She listened to me carefully and decided that Anthony should have a psychiatric evaluation. She then recommended a pediatric psychiatrist with 31 years of experience in providing specialized services for children with developmental disorders. I felt very fortunate to have such a patient, distinguished and well qualified doctor assess my son. Without this professional's input, I would never have been able to navigate this *Alice-in-Wonderland-like* system known as "special-ed" so skillfully all these years.

As time went by, I realized that Anthony's days at that school had to come to an end. It just wasn't working out for anyone. Every day presented us with new difficulties, and it became intolerable for me as a mother, never knowing what new horror would occur. We made it all the way through to spring; April 1st would be his final day. Yet even so, I received a phone call early that morning, advising me to pick him up immediately. It was absolutely clear that he was no longer welcome there. It was time to start down a new path.

His teacher had tried her best to keep him in her class, but the administration had different ideas altogether. I will always remember that she had had his best interests at heart and for that, she will always have a special place in *my* heart. He was out of school 71 days that year, not a good situation for any child.

After all the evaluations, it was decided that the best place for him in the coming September would be at the local school for special needs children. I kept my fingers crossed, prayed a lot, and hoped that this choice would work for him and our family. Only time would tell.

Chapter 18
"Ignorance is Bliss"
The Costco Fiasco

It was a typical hot day in the summer when Anthony Jr. was five years old, and Michael was three. My husband suggested a trip to Costco for some bulk shopping and a change of scene. As a mother of young children, I knew that such a venture could go either way, but I also realized that my husband wanted to get out of the house to lose himself among the tools and man cave accessories. For my part, I would have preferred going to the dentist for a tooth extraction rather than trekking over to Costco, which is usually jam-packed with shopping carts that are pushed by rude shoppers with tunnel vision, especially when my sons are with me.

At this stage in our lives, my husband still wanted to believe that we were a typical family of four going on a shopping run. However, I could have easily predicted from recent experiences that this trip was not a good idea. Against my better judgment though, my husband was able to convince me that we needed to stock up for the summer barbeque season with frozen meats, drinks, snacks, condiments, etc.... I gave in, simply because it was too hot to argue, and because maybe, just maybe, I was being too cautious.

So, we packed the children in the car with some goldfish snacks and boxed drinks. We started singing, "How Much is That Doggie in the Window?" They both loved that song so we sang it over and over again until before we knew it, we had arrived. My husband went to grab a wagon, while I unbuckled the boys from their seats. I suddenly noticed that Anthony Jr.'s eyes were glazed over and he appeared listless, but I decided to ignore these tell-tale signs, telling myself that once he was in the store, he would be just fine.

Upon entering the store, we headed for the meat section to pick up some chicken cutlets, steaks, hamburgers, and hot dogs. Immediately afterwards, we went to the breakfast aisle where I searched for Cheerios among what seemed like hundreds of cereal boxes piled from ceiling to floor. All of the sudden, Anthony Jr. started to grow restless and began fidgeting and fussing like most children his age, but then his behavior progressed into a major meltdown, which is more dramatic than a childish temper tantrum. An older couple walked by and I could see that the woman was annoyed with my son's uncontrollable outburst. Every parent knows the repercussions of such a public display by a child: the shoppers staring with disapproval, coupled with your own anxiety and embarrassment, not to mention that feeling of utter helplessness.

My husband saw that Michael was also getting nervous, so he picked him up to comfort him. I followed his example by taking Anthony Jr. into my arms and sat us down together on a huge crate so I could rub his back and calm him down. Remember that older couple? As they passed us by, the woman snidely said, "If he was my kid, I'd give him a beating!" My husband knew what was coming. He put Michael in the wagon, and I handed him Anthony Jr. I glared back at her and retorted, "Thank God he's not your son! My son has a disability. So, what's your excuse?" The man appeared to be mortified by his wife's actions.

Of course, at this point I really wanted to go home and forget about how ignorance is bliss. Once I had confirmed that Anthony Jr. had calmed down, I agreed to continue shopping for our supplies. I understood now that my older son would get very overwhelmed in certain places because of his processing delays. Next, he would feel frustrated by not being able to understand his own emotions, and then become further anguished at not being able to clearly communicate his distress with us. (Hell, I get overwhelmed in certain places!) I heard Anthony sigh wistfully,

"Mommy, my stomach is telling me I'm hungry."

So that was why he was crying! That stranger wanted me to beat my child because she lacked the imagination to see that he was hungry, had trouble expressing it, and was developmentally delayed. I hoped that the Costco Granny was not a real grandmother because God help her grandchildren if they ever misbehaved!

We took the boys to the concession stand where we sat and fed the boys. As I went for a refill of my fountain drink, I saw Costco Granny's husband. He wanted to apologize for her. I politely thanked him for his decency but told him to advise his wife that she should keep her thoughts to herself because you can never know the circumstances surrounding a situation. My advice to everyone reading this is that when you see someone struggling with a child - any child - anywhere, simply ask if you can help in any way. Why do you need to judge? Offer your assistance instead of your opinion. At this point in time, our society should be well aware of the heartbreak of a parent that has a child with special needs. You would be amazed at what that parents' reaction would be to the kindness you extend towards them, instead of the usual stares and derision they have sadly come to expect.

After this long, distressful day, the boys were placed in bed. I received a phone call from my friend Laura, my neighbor who lives down the block. She wanted to know if I would like to hang out and watch a movie. She is my "girly" girlfriend, the one who always knows how bargain shopping and picking out great accessories would perk up her pal when she was having a very bad day. She was that person for me, the one whose door was always open for a cup of coffee, a quick lunch, or a heart-to-heart chat. (On top of everything, she was also a very good listener!)

Well, tonight I really needed to have some adult conversation with my friend, while eating some sweet-and-salty snacks and watching "The Notebook." (By the way, it's a great chick flick.) She asked how my day had gone, and I started venting about our Costco run, knowing that Laura would be the voice of enlightenment. She came through as usual, telling me,

"People like that need your prayers, not your anger. You should feel sorry for them because they don't know any better. Do they?"

I understood that I needed to stop being resentful and start heeding my girlfriend's advice. Her advice made me realize that people are only human and usually find it difficult to understand the problems that others face on a daily basis.

That night I prayed for the Costco Granny, her husband, and others like them. I prayed that, for the sake of my son and his fellow sufferers, humanity's hearts may be filled with love, empathy and compassion. I asked God to give them the gift of insight to truly see what was in front of them without passing judgment. Amen.

Chapter 19
"Community Nursery School"
All by Myself

In September of 2001, Anthony Jr. had just entered nursery school. I will never forget his first day of school. My stomach was sick with the fear of knowing how difficult the separation was going to be for both of us, even though it was only for a few hours in the afternoon, three days a week.

His two nursery school teachers were quick to notice that Anthony Jr. had developmental delays. I wanted to believe his slow progress was caused by his epilepsy, but deep down I knew it was more than that. As a young, scared mother, I was struck by their commitment as well as by their support. A few years later, when Michael attended the school, one of these same teachers actually potty trained him, a milestone that I thought was never going to happen. Anthony was potty trained at twenty months, but Michael just didn't want to get out of those diapers! This dedicated teacher took on that task like a proud mama and succeeded.

While Anthony had some good days, there were some days that were not so good and, on those days, I received phone calls. He was frustrated with himself because he had a hard time socializing with children his age. Yet, despite the uphill battle, his two teachers continued working with him.

On the days I was called into the school, I would find Anthony in the director's office. He was sent there whenever he needed a break from the classroom, and she would place him on her lap and play games with him. She would sing with him, and give him coloring books, action figures and puzzles for amusement. She was the sweetest, most loving, and compassionate person that I met at the beginning of Anthony's school days. She always knew what he truly wanted, whether it was a snack, a drink, a hug, a song, or just a bit of one-on-one quality time. She delivered just that. He loved being in her office with her, all by himself.

Although I was confused and frustrated with Anthony's apparent discomfort inside the classroom, I felt quite comfortable with his placement at that school. His safety was never a concern for me; it was his inability to make friends, or to recognize letters and numbers that concerned me. No matter how many flash cards and learning games I tried out with him, Anthony just couldn't remember or retain what we had just gone over a few minutes earlier. All that practice only heightened my concerns and fears. *What was wrong with my son???*

At the age of two, Anthony would play and socialize at *Tots on Track*, but when I left him alone in the play area with the other children, he would cry and hold his breath until he was blue. This behavior began at a *Mommy and Me* session when the children separated from their parents to play with their peers. Moreover, Anthony had a lot of difficulty sitting still, playing with others, and following rules. So, from the very beginning, it was obvious that he was not developing at the same pace as the other children his age.

To look at him, you would never be able to see that anything could possibly be "wrong" or "abnormal." Yet, I knew that something was not right when I saw how he struggled with simple tasks that came so easily for other children. Those were the dark days, the days of self-doubt, self-pity, and rage.

At the same time, my mom had been diagnosed with uterine cancer and needed a full hysterectomy. The circumstances surrounding her diagnosis were indeed miraculous. Thank God she came through unscathed because I am not quite sure what I would do without her. She is the matriarch and a great support to my children and family. It wasn't always that way, but it is now. I am forever grateful for her.

Chapter 20
"Am I Going to Die?"
My Diagnosis with Graves' Disease

After Michael's birth in June of 2001, I felt my body was not healthy. My hands were always shaking and my hair was falling out. I was deeply depressed and sometimes unable to catch my breath. My skin was constantly burning, my weight loss was ongoing, and my bowels were loose. These symptoms continued for months. I knew something had to be wrong, but I ignored my instincts.

The truth was that my worries over my son Anthony not only clouded my judgment, but also intensified my fears. I really didn't want to know what was wrong with me; I just hoped everything would get better on its own. I finally heeded the advice of close friends who had been urging me to take some kind of action and went to see my primary care physician. His diagnosis was "anxiety due to the September 11th attacks." I tried to explain that what I was feeling was more than just anxiety. He prescribed Buspar, which I never took. I never realized that things could go from bad to worse in an instant.

Three months passed with no significant improvement. One morning, I went to the gym for my usual workout; the last thing I remembered was cycling with five minutes to go. In a nano-second, my heart began racing and I blacked out. Needless to say, that episode scared me into reality. If something were to happen to me, who would raise my children and advocate for them?

I went straight to the doctor's office for an emergency appointment. It was time for a second opinion. I followed my intuition and requested a blood test for autoimmune disease. The blood results revealed that I had something called "Graves' Disease," an autoimmune disorder that affects the thyroid. I had a large goiter, with high levels of thyroid hormone that were attacking my heart and vital organs. I learned that Graves' disease causes the body to produce antibodies to the receptor for thyroid-stimulating hormone (TSH).

I was referred to an endocrinologist who specialized in glands and diseases of the glands. He ran more tests and explained that doctors don't like to remove the thyroid unless necessary. He prescribed Propranolol, which is a beta blocker that blocks the effects of hormones on the body and Methimazole (or Thiamazole), an anti-thyroid medication. Seemingly endless months of uncertainty, irritability, anxiety and frustration followed this diagnosis. Of course, I wanted to get better yesterday, but I knew my recovery would most likely be a much longer process than I wanted it to be.

In fact, I was on medication for approximately four years until I was given a radioactive iodine treatment in February 2005. With this therapy, you take radioactive iodine (or radioiodine) by mouth. The thyroid needs iodine to produce hormones, so it consumes the radioiodine, which then destroys the overactive thyroid cells over time. The hoped-for outcome was that my thyroid gland would slowly begin to shrink, and the symptoms to gradually decrease within several weeks to several months.

Unfortunately, I needed two doses of radioactive iodine because in my case, one dose was not enough (*naturally!*). Torture me, why don't you? What made matters worse was that I needed to stay at my parents' home in their basement because I could not be near my children for at least three days.

I decided since I was marooned there, I might as well make good use of my time. I asked my mom to put highlights in my hair, which she had done before on many occasions. However, this time, she left the highlights in for so long that I turned into a platinum blonde. (I have jet black hair.) All I wanted was a few highlights to cover the grey! When I looked in the mirror, I was traumatized. My mother didn't know what to say. Her first response was, "Oh my God!" She followed with, "Don't worry-hair grows." After that, who needed to look in the mirror? Until then, I thought my hairstylist could correct my mother's handiwork. Not really! Whenever anyone would see me, their first questions were all about my hair, not my health. I could not conceive what they were thinking. Some of them even thought it was a side effect of the radioactive iodine.

After that second dose of radioactive iodine and follow-up thyroid medications, my levels gradually became close to normal. Thyroid disease is more serious than it sounds since the thyroid controls your body temperature, weight, thinking, nervous system and other organs. In short, if your thyroid is off, everything else is off, too.

A word to the wise: Don't ignore signs when your body is trying to tell you something is wrong. I was playing chess with Death and he was winning. My friends and family pushed me to take care of myself. Without them, I probably wouldn't be here.

Chapter 21
"My Eventful Trip to Target"
The Arrival of Michael

It was June 2001 and I had two weeks of waiting until our second son was to be born. Anyone who has been pregnant knows that towards the end of your last trimester, you just want the baby out! To make matters worse, it was the beginning of those hot summer days and I was waddling around, tired and swollen. My condition, however, did not stop me from shopping with my mom at Target for a few extra baby supplies.

We arrived at Target in the late afternoon because it was just too stifling earlier in the day to do much of anything. As we walked towards the store, I told my mom that I was feeling a lot of pressure below…and then unwisely pushed the thought out of my head.

I had my list of various baby needs and slowly hobbled about the store picking up various items (t-shirts, diapers, bibs, burping cloths, pajamas etc.). As I checked off the last few items on my list, I turned to look at the shopping cart and it was gone. I looked around in disbelief that someone had taken my wagon. So, I started to roam the aisles to search for it, but to no avail; my cart filled with my precious baby items was nowhere to be found. I was fit to be tied! After all, I was nine months pregnant, and in no condition to be wandering around a store that I had just purposefully made my way around already!

Then suddenly, to make matters even worse, I felt a tingling wet sensation. This was strange, but in my present mood, I thought nothing of it. My mom was telling me to relax, but stubborn creature that I am, I continued on my mission. We went to security to ask them to page customers to see if anyone had "mistakenly" taken a wagon with baby items. However, no sooner was the announcement made, that my water broke! Yep, that was the wet tingling sensation. My mom's sound advice was to leave the items and come back for them later. I argued with her, sarcastically asking "When? When the baby is born? After all this? No! I don't think so!" At that point, my wagon was returned by a customer who hadn't realized her mistake. I was extremely impatient and hormonal. All I kept thinking was about how the customer had a wagon full of baby items. How could she not notice? Soon after, we paid for all the baby items and went to my parents' home.

At 11:31 pm that night, Michael came into the world via C-section… two weeks earlier than anticipated. My second prince had come into the world. Just when I thought my heart wasn't big enough to love another child unconditionally, I was proven wrong.

Chapter 22
"It's Time!"
The Arrival of Anthony, Jr.

Nine months had passed, and I was consumed with the worry and fear of not only becoming a new parent, but also the thoughts of how this baby would affect our fledgling marriage. We had conceived the child on the first night of our honeymoon and so were still considered newlyweds. As most newly married couples, we were trying to become accustomed to living together under the same roof, and now we also needed to adjust to parenthood – both in such a short period of time!

It was October 15, 1998… I remember very vividly standing in my kitchen barefoot and pregnant, wondering if this would be the day for the arrival of our son. I was barefoot because even my most lived-in shoes no longer fit comfortably on my swollen feet. My belly was so extended that I could no longer see those swollen feet or bend down to put closed shoes on. UGH! All I kept thinking was *Let today be the day!*

I hadn't really slept the night before because it was so difficult to get comfortable, and most of the time I suffered with acid reflux. Throughout my pregnancy I suffered with morning sickness. In reality, for me it was morning, noon, and night sickness. My husband would constantly find me in the bathroom with my head in the bowl. In retrospect, I don't really think my husband had a clue as to what I was going through since my hormones were fluctuating and my body was constantly changing. No matter how many books you read, nothing can ever prepare you for any of this.

As I think back on that beautiful October day, I remember folding laundry in my kitchen, feeling quite uncomfortable due to the pressure inflicted on my spine while standing. At 5:00 pm, a pain so indescribably sharp and intense took hold of my body. I thought to myself that this had to be the anxiously anticipated beginning of the so-called contractions! I called my husband at work to let him know my contractions had started. He asked if I was OK, and then told me in a very gentle voice that he loved me and we would soon be parents.

He arrived from work that evening around 7:15 pm and kissed me and my belly. We decided to go to the diner that was within walking distance so he could eat. Even though my discomfort was growing, I decided to eat toast with a cup of chicken noodle soup.

We arrived at the hospital around 8:45 pm and I was admitted to the obstetrics floor. The nurse gave me a hospital gown and asked that I walk around the hospital to help induce labor. Unfortunately, after walking an hour with ever increasing pain, there was no progress. After what seemed like forever, they finally took us into the family birthing room. My mom asked to stay with us, and I was very pleased that she did.

My doctor broke my water and my son defecated inside of me. This is known as Meconium Aspiration. Approximately 15 minutes later, I vomited all over the doctor's fashionable Armani shoes. (I guess that's why they tell you not to eat before giving birth, but really - what was he thinking by wearing such expensive shoes in that room in the first place???) I continued to push and push for many hours with no significant progress. My husband was so exhausted from working all day and being with me through these pain-filled hours of labor; I was fortunate to have my mom in the birthing room with me. At one point, I told her something was very wrong. I knew my baby was stuck because I could feel him lodged behind my hips. She immediately understood the danger and told the doctor that if he didn't take the baby from me *right now*, she would either lose me, her grandson, or both of us.

The specialist confirmed my mother's instructions: my son was not to be born naturally but by C-section because I had a genetic disorder that prevented my hips from expanding while giving birth. The delivery room was prepped, and I gave birth on October 16th at approximately 6:54 am to Anthony Jr. My husband cried as he held his son for the first time. As they put him on my chest, I experienced the unique sensation of being a mother. All the agony, fear, and anxiety were forgotten. My entire family was given the news in the waiting area and my mom could finally breathe easily.

The next day my parents saw their grandson for the first time. I noticed that my mother's face was ashen, but in the fog of optimism that a new baby always brings, I decided it was due to her lack of sleep. Anthony Jr. was sleeping in the hospital basinet, so we waited patiently for his feeding time. My dad had gone to the cafeteria for some coffee and rolls. Finally, my prince awakened and I handed him over to my mom. As she cradled her grandson in her arms for the first time, she collapsed on my bed. I forced myself to ignore my initial shock and rang the buzzer for the nurses' desk. As soon as the nurse arrived, I screamed that something was wrong with my mom. She was quickly placed in a wheelchair and taken to the emergency room for tests.

I was a brand-new mom and now my mom was in intensive care a few floors below me. I could not seem to wrap my head around any of it. It was just incredible. Was this really happening? I wanted desperately to see her but was prevented from doing because she had had a nuclear medical test. Since this quarantine was just a precautionary measure, the next day I decided to take matters into my own hands.

Despite the warnings and my being in recovery for my C-section, I slowly walked over to the next wing and took the elevator down. As I was congratulating myself on my gutsy initiative, the fire alarm sounded, the elevator stopped in between floors, and the water sprinklers went off. Now what? So much drama! This is what I got for not obeying the rules! About 20 minutes later, the sprinklers stopped and the elevator inched its way down to the lobby. Great! I was soaking wet in my silky green pajamas, and I had to get back to the maternity ward to feed my son and make sure my mom was fine in the middle of all of this chaos.

I eventually made my way back to maternity, only to be scolded by the head nurse for my misdeeds. I also found out that my mom had indeed had a heart attack due to both the excitement and lack of sleep over the birth of her grandson. I was actually released a day before my mom. All turned out alright for everyone all those years ago. Yet, I should have known from the very beginning that the intensity of my son's entry into the world would foretell the drama to follow!

FOR MY PARENTS

A Mother's Intuition:
Autism – A Journey into Forgiveness
& Healing Continues…

Written By: Catherine Marinelli – Gagliano
As told by: Linda Pedreira

Do not walk a mile in my shoes.

Rather, reach a milestone in my shoes.

Only then will you understand that

my journey isn't about length and distance;

it's about strength and persistence.

www.nationalautismassociation.org

LOOKING FORWARD

What follows this first chapter of the sequel to *A Mother's Intuition* are the starts and stops, the triumphs and tragedies, and the supports and oppositions I have lived through during the years that followed as my journey continued. The bonds of friendships, both old and new, have been a constant source of strength, and yet, paradoxically, the resistances that were hurled at me from unexpected sources also fortified my resolve to continue onwards, both for my family and for myself.

Volume II

Chapter 1
"A New Beginning"
Bariatric Surgery and Transformation

The day had finally come, July 28, 2014. I had been keeping my future bariatric surgery to myself, husband, and spiritual teacher Terry for approximately one year. I may not have looked it, but my weight had ballooned to about 300 pounds. Terry was truly worried for my well-being, and used many conversations to dissuade me, but I was determined. She took on the role of devil's advocate. She wanted me to seriously think about the fact that the procedure could not be reversed, and that it would permanently alter my body. She spoke about the side effects and reminded me again and again that the road ahead would be challenging.

Through years of stress-eating and raising our two autistic sons, I was not physically healthy. I had unregulated sugar issues, high blood pressure, some depression, and anxiety. Something needed to change so I could be around for my family.

Growing up, my weight always fluctuated, and as I grew older, that habit still hadn't changed. I am certain I had an undiagnosed eating disorder and was an emotional binge-eater. As in every family, there was a certain amount of dysfunction. When the adults around you cannot seem to comprehend that their actions (such as emotional abuse) and their negative behaviors have consequences, their children end up suffering with low self-esteem, anxiety, depression and loneliness. Sometimes these parents never received the emotional support and skills themselves when they were growing up, and in turn, do not know how to raise their children any differently. It's really up to you as an adult to recognize those repeated negative patterns. Work on yourself and heal that childhood trauma, so that you can become a better parent and adult to break that cycle.

To become a successful, well-rounded person, your emotional IQ is very important in many aspects of life. What is emotional IQ? Emotional intelligence (otherwise known as emotional quotient or EQ) is the ability to understand, use, and manage your own emotions in positive ways to relieve stress, communicate effectively, empathize with others, overcome challenges and defuse conflict.[i]

I have done this work on myself for many years - spiritually, mentally, and emotionally. The physical portion has always been the biggest challenge, exemplified by my struggles with my weight. It is all about making lifestyle changes and dealing with emotions to succeed with long-term goals.

To prepare myself for bariatric surgery, I met with many health professionals and underwent many tests: a cardiologist for the heart, an endocrinologist for my thyroid, a nutritionist for healthy eating, and a psychiatrist for mental and emotional issues. Honestly, if you do not clear away your emotional damage before undergoing this type of surgery, you will most likely not be as successful as you could be. You will replace overeating with other bad habits, such as alcoholism, overspending, gambling, etc. I have watched others go through this process to lose weight, but have not worked on these deep-rooted issues, and so they look for other coping mechanisms to feel better. However, that behavior just makes you feel worse.

I had my bariatric surgery (gastric sleeve) in 2014. Sleeve gastrectomy is a surgical weight-loss procedure in which the stomach is reduced to about 15% of its original size, by surgical removal of a large portion of the stomach along the greater curvature. The result is a sleeve or tube-like structure.[ii] I dropped115 pounds in six months. I also lost half of my hair, which completely traumatized me, and I did not feel healthy. Looking at my new body in the mirror felt good, but I didn't feel well physically. I vomited often and was unable to keep food down. I had to learn to cut my food into small pieces, chew slowly, and drink only after I ate. Until this day, I need to take a regimen of vitamins, and make sure I am getting enough nutrients. I have issues drinking plain water, and never feel really full because of my decreased stomach size. There is also a consistently irritating inflammation of my stomach if I eat too quickly or intake too many carbohydrates. My insides flutter every time I eat, which gives me anxiety, but I have learned to adapt. The surgery is only a tool, so you need to implement lifelong changes, which are not always easy.

I gained some weight since my father's passing and during the pandemic, but I have kept a majority of it off. I am acutely aware that this slight setback is due to my emotions, hormonal imbalances, and my being perimenopausal. As an adult woman, I am learning to accept and love my curves. It is all about perspective, self-love, and what you project to others. I am what you could call a *work in progress*. There is always something to learn. It is a never-ending process. If you do not perform the inside work, your former self creeps up and bursts out in so many unhealthy ways. The loving relationship we have with ourselves must come first in order for our other relationships to flourish, be healthy, and succeed.

This chapter was a very difficult one because I had to expose my vulnerability, and honestly reveal my flaws and struggles as a person. No one is perfect. The only way we can make positive change is to admit there are changes that need to be made.

[i] www.helpguide.org
[ii] **www.mayoclinic.org**

Chapter 2
"Honored at the Muttontown Country Club"
Our Trip to Antigua

It was an evening to remember, Thursday, December 4, 2014. I was being honored for my work in the special needs community and for my book *A Mother's Intuition*. Every year a fundraiser is held and that year it was the 56th Annual Dinner. I was chosen as the honoree by the CDD Board of Directors. After all we had been through as a family, here was a memorable evening of gratitude, love, laughter, and healing. My parents, siblings, the CDD Board of Directors, its staff, and the families of the Center for Developmental Disabilities were going to be in attendance.

Nick Boba was Managing Director at the time. He was a kind, gentle leader, wise man, and a mentor to many, including myself. He believed and practiced Buddhism, and I always found meeting with him to be insightful and fascinating. We believed in the same things and paid it forward. I think about him often and miss his gentle energy. We would sit in his office and discuss so many things, including the meaning of life and the soul's purpose here on earth. A few hours spent with Nick felt like mere minutes. I refer to this as *traveling down the rabbit hole* in *Alice in Wonderland*. What was time? When speaking with like-minded individuals, time feels nonlinear and magical. We are all connected by energy and events, some of which are unexplainable. This happens to me quite often with certain special individuals in my life.

I had gone shopping with my mom a month before the fundraiser. We purchased a beautiful long black gown and my mom bought me stunning gold sparkling shoes. I felt like a princess. When I was five years old, I would wear my Cinderella gown, hold my magical wand, and grant everyone's wishes. How those core memories stay with us.

My husband and I had been at odds with my parents since putting Anthony in residential placement, but now I was sharing the showers of happiness and gratitude with them. My parents were so proud and accepting of our decisions now, as they witnessed and experienced Anthony's successes, growth potential and independence. It took quite some time, hard work, patience, and sacrifice to get to this point, but now here we were, and my heart was full.

The Muttontown Country Club's Grand Ballroom was packed. I was in awe at the amount of people and the exciting energy in the room. We were going to raise lots of money for the children and distribute many generous gifts to those in attendance.

I had written a speech that I was to deliver before the festivities began. Public speaking was always difficult for me, but this night was all about giving back and celebrating a common cause. As expected, my heart was racing in my chest as I stepped up to the podium, but it was different this time. I felt the presence of peace, my angels were with me, and my words inspired the attendees. Some were moved to laughter, and some responded with tears. I received a standing ovation. Our fundraiser was a big success! My family and I were presented with round-trip tickets to Antigua and a week's stay at the Verandah Resort and Spa. I was so elated and grateful that sleep would not come easily that night. My brain was in high gear, planning our future trip.

We had made plans for the following year, departing on July 11, 2015, staying at the resort for a week. On that highly anticipated morning, we were picked up by limousine and taken to JFK Airport. My sons followed all the protocols and directions with no difficulties. The flights, landings, navigation through the airport, and transportation to the resort all went off without a hitch. Usually there would be a meltdown or two before arriving at any place while traveling. We were so extremely fortunate this time. Our son AJ who had not lived with us since he was seven-and-a-half-years-old was now seventeen and very independent. My husband and I had a serious decision to make because we wanted to stay at the resort, whereas AJ wanted to go out and experience the entire island. AJ was soon introduced to the activities director who had his own disability - one of his arms and hands were shorter in length and smaller than the other. I explained to my husband we needed to let him go and be that independent young man we were raising him to be. Both my husband and AJ's brother Michael, who was fourteen years old at the time, disagreed with me. If you ask me, I am sure it was their nerves and anxiety about allowing AJ to explore this unfamiliar place.

Every morning AJ would meet the activities director after breakfast, and follow the activities agenda with all the other guests - volleyball, hiking, touring, tennis, water sports, etc. He would meet us for lunch and afternoon medications, and then return to the cottage at 6:30 pm in time for dinner. I showed him the availability of the phones in every section of the resort and how to use them to call a cart for transportation. I assured him not to panic if he became lost, since all of the cottages looked alike. To proactively circumvent that possibility, he wore his name and cottage ID around his neck and was given an emergency $20.00.

I told my husband to let AJ experience the island through his own eyes. If we held him back, the trip would not be the same for him. One morning he awoke, took his meds, and went for a walk. He followed a man cutting fruits off the island trees. Two hours later, he knocked on the door with a cut -open coconut and two mangoes. With excitement in his voice, he exclaimed, "Mom, I wanted you to taste a real fresh coconut cut off from the tree!"

My husband argued that there had to be something wrong with me to let him go out on his own like that, but I knew it was time and that he was ready. I told my husband to hang out at the pool, enjoy some drinks, let go, and let GOD take the wheel. Don't misunderstand me…I was just as nervous, but I had faith in the power of prayer - and this was the time to implement it. I asked AJ's angels to guide, love, and protect him every day, and to safely return him to us unharmed and happy. That's exactly what happened.

All in all, it was an awesome trip! By the end of it, all the tourists and island natives knew who he was and greeted him with a smile and a hello! The young man who had struggled to communicate in the past, had now become the island's most popular visitor.

Chapter 3
"My Boys Make Confirmation" My Parents, Their Sponsors

I will start this chapter by saying, *"It is amazing how situations can be turned around with unconditional love, patience, and understanding in our relationships."* As you know from my first book, my relationship with my traditional Italian parents had become strained due to our placing Anthony in a residential program. It was such a heart-wrenching decision, made more difficult by how some family and a few friends could not relate at all. For anyone to believe Anthony's move made our lives easier, they were just wrong in every way.

Michael was then in second grade, and diagnosed with Asperger's Syndrome, which is a developmental disorder affecting one's ability to effectively socialize and communicate. It is a condition on the autism spectrum, with generally higher functioning. People with this condition may be socially awkward and have an all-absorbing interest in specific topics. Communication training and behavioral therapy can help people with the syndrome learn to socialize more successfully.[i] Faced with this diagnosis, I felt that it was important for me to become a catechist. It would put both my sons' anxieties at ease since, for Anthony, it was a given that I would have to be his religious instructor, and for Michael, he would need a familiar presence like me to make him feel more comfortable. Moreover, as their teacher, the classes took place in our home. Yet, despite all of these factors, I knew this would be no simple task.

I went to St. Rose of Lima Parish and had myself listed with the religious education office. A few days later, I received the emails of the students to be in the class, four boys and four girls, which included my son Michael. Our son Anthony would be taught religion on the weekends when he came home, so that he could receive Confirmation with his brother and classmates.

During the years of religious instruction, I would express how important it was to accept and love others unconditionally, to be kind, to give to the community, and to those in need. I told my students that God was everywhere, not only in the Catholic church, and that God lived inside each and every one of us and so the church was us. *"We are the church."* The church is the Christian religious community as a whole, or a body or organization of Christian believers. Christians will express their faith on Sundays and religious holidays, which is when most Christians attend mass. The Mass itself is a central liturgical rite in the Catholic Church encompassing the Word of God and consecration of the Holy Eucharist.[ii]

Most Christians attend mass in search of God and peace within themselves. I feel inner work needs to happen in order to find peace along with daily acts of kindness. Attending mass should only amplify that peace within ourselves. Some always attend mass, but outside the church do "NOT" behave as true Christians at all. My goal in teaching these children was integrity, behavior and how you should treat your fellow human beings. This says more about your character than attending mass. Man created the churches and wrote the Bible. Jesus preached to the poor and to anyone that would listen while standing on dirt, with no pews, or glass-stained windows, and for whom the pursuit of riches was not a priority. That is what Christianity means. You should never be afraid of God for he is forgiving and emanates everlasting love. This is what I believe and practice every day.

Now I had the opportunity to teach these precepts to my religious ed class to inspire them to do good with their lives. It wasn't always easy to read from the workbook and Bible and put those teachings in terms that these younger minds could understand and interpret for themselves. They were so inquisitive and full of questions, and I was fortunate enough to be a part of their religious growth.

On occasion, we would attend church and say the rosary as a group. We would also participate in activities, such as donating supplies to the needy, and discussing what had been expected of them throughout the years - up until when they were ready to make their Confirmation. They were a sincere, loving, and compassionate group. I cared for each one of their different personalities and for what they brought to the table each week.

As their Confirmation approached, I waited patiently to see whom my children would pick to be their sponsors. Anthony immediately said he was going to ask my dad, his Grandpa Armando, to be his sponsor. To my delight, Michael wanted my mom, Grandma Angela, to be his. I held back my tears of excitement and joy. All of the trials and tribulations we had been through over the years as a family had come full circle in a loving gesture from my boys to my parents. In my life, I have always chosen forgiveness and love. I had worked diligently on my relationship with my parents, and this was a full testament of those efforts.

The day my boys and students received the Holy Spirit and Confirmation was October 28th, 2015, and it was such a proud moment for me. Watching my parents place their hands on my sons as they received their sacrament was a memorable gift. I recall being in awe, sitting in the pew and saying to myself, *"Please God, continue to guide, love, and protect my sons and students on their journey of life, for I have done my best in my small part of teaching them to always shine their light brightly and to always make good decisions."*

That afternoon we celebrated with a few family members and friends. My heart was full of gratitude and pride. Our sons had reached another milestone, and my parents were a central part of that. Who would have thought that it would turn out the way it did? I felt truly blessed as we sat at the table, broke bread, and drank wine. We are and always will be family.

It was a bittersweet time for all of us, but especially for me. Throughout the years, I would have these children in my home at least once a week. Now that they had made their Confirmation, our visits would end. Up until this day, I wonder how those years flew by so quickly. I follow most of the students on social media, and I continue to be completely proud of them and their accomplishments. Life goes by so fast…I am honored to have been a small part of their journey.

[i] www.mayoclinic.org
[ii] www.gotQuestions.org

Chapter 4
"My Forever Friend Patty"
My Hero

My best friend Patty and I usually speak in the morning while having a cup of coffee, and then again at night to discuss our day and whatever else comes to mind. She is my ride-or-die and soul sister who knows where all the bodies are buried, so to speak. We connect telepathically throughout the day and through our twenty-four years of friendship. She and her husband are godparents to our youngest son Michael. We are very fortunate and blessed because they have become second parents to both of our sons throughout the years. She is definitely one of the most intelligent women that I know. Patty is strong in every way, calls it the way she sees it, sincere, loving, full of faith, and very compassionate. Patty pulls me back from the edge. We are a lot alike.

During one of our many phone calls in March of 2016, Patty was not herself. I felt it as our conversation began. Patty explained that she had health concerns for her mom. Throughout the years, she has spent a lot of quality time with her mom. Anne had lost her husband, Patty's dad, who passed years ago to Melanoma. Charles was also the love of Anne's life. Previously, Patty had noticed her mom had no appetite, was losing weight, and had bowel issues. Her sister would cook food and it would be found sitting untouched in the fridge. Patty confided in me that she made an appointment for her mom to have tests done the following month in St. Joseph's Hospital in Bethpage. I had a sinking feeling in the pit of my stomach. My friend and I feared that the news wasn't going to be good, but we both prayed and tried to remain positive.

The following month her mom was diagnosed with Colorectal Cancer. (Cancer of the colon and rectum). She called me from the hospital with the devastating news. I immediately drove there to support my friend. The doctor advised us that Anne needed to have surgery immediately. She also informed us that after the colon reconstructive surgery, Anne would most likely have a colonoscopy bag. This was so heartbreaking. Anne had the surgery, underwent many months of radiation, and still lost her battle on September 4, 2018, in her home surrounded by family. Beautiful, loving Anne was now in heaven with her husband Charles. Anne had always given me the love, support, and strength I needed - especially when making decisions for our son Anthony and his residential placement. I will never forget the love she shared with me and my sons.

It was a few days after Anne had passed away that I had a vision from Patty's dad, Charles. He was a military police officer for the Army. He's visited me a few times before, but this time it was a little different: Handsome Charles with his serious, deep blue eyes, round defined face, and tall broad shoulders, wearing a black leather jacket and beret. His energy was heavy and anxious, and thus I knew this visitation was connected to Patty. He thanked me for being a good friend to his daughter, and for paying attention to her because he was concerned.

It was September 7th, the day of Anne's funeral. My family and I attended with my parents. On the way in, we gave our condolences to the family, and I sat with Patty for a while. She did not look good at all. Loss takes its toll on us physically, emotionally, and mentally. Considering her mom had just passed, I was trying not to think the worst, but her father's words rang in my ears. Intuitively, I knew something was brewing. My dad then whispered in my ear that Patty didn't look well, and she was too pale. I asked her how she was feeling. She explained that her leg was red and swollen.

The following week, I had my weekly appointment with my spiritual healer and friend Terry. We spoke of my concerns for Patty, and she confirmed that it was for valid reasons. Terry and I had had a discussion two years prior in 2016 that there would be a serious health struggle for Patty. I prayed for her many days and nights. I kept it to myself, although it bothered me tremendously. What good would it do to mention it? As time passed, I always thought it would be a problem with blood to the brain or a blood clot. At least that was the message from spirit - not always accurate, but close enough.

For months. Patty had been going to Weight Watchers, swimming, and exercising, but still gaining weight. She was eating healthy foods in small portions, so this made no sense to me. Patty had always been self-conscious about her weight. She was on disability and had been diagnosed with a foot drop, diabetic cellulitis, which turned into neuropathy. She needed to walk either with a cane or walker. (Foot drop, or drop foot, is a general term for difficulty lifting the front part of the foot.) If you have a foot drop, the front of your foot might drag on the ground when you walk. Foot drop isn't a disease, but rather a sign of an underlying neurological, muscular or anatomical problem. Peripheral neuropathy, a result of damage to the nerves located outside of the brain and spinal cord (peripheral nerves), often causes weakness, numbness and pain, usually in the hands and feet. It can also affect other areas and body functions including digestion, urination and circulation.[i] Yet, Patty continued her quest to be very independent, and rely on no one.

In her position at the bank, Patty often worked with Homeland Security. She would follow wired money from terrorists or other groups and freeze their accounts and assets. Patty could balance money in accounts within seconds, to the penny and without a calculator. Throughout those many years, she was suffering from hypoglycemia and anemia. She had no idea that these conditions would gravely affect her health after 9/11.

On August 14, 2003, while in my parents' swimming pool, I had a sharp feeling about Patty. I envisioned her stuck in an elevator. I searched for news on my cell phone and saw that there was a blackout occurring in New York City. I called her office and asked for Patricia Eberstein. The woman on the phone said, "She's not at her desk. May I take a message and get back to you?" I waited 30 minutes before I called back. I received no satisfactory answers.

Two long hours passed, and now I began calling her family members. I left a message for her husband, and then spoke to her aunt to explain that I believed Patty was in trouble. After reaching Patty's supervisor at home, she explained that Patty had been missing for hours and had never made it back to her desk. The bank manager had assumed she had made it down to the street, and then left to go home. That would be out of character for her. I asked them to look in her desk, and her purse was still there. The bank called in the fire department for a search. My best friend had been stuck in an elevator for eight hours alone with a single light and broken emergency phone and camera. Her father had been an elevator mechanic and I am sure he was with her there in spirit - and kept that light on for her. No one at the bank had any idea she was stuck in that elevator, but I had remained relentless, telling them to keep searching because if not, I was going to drive into New York City and find my best friend myself!

The firemen called down the elevator shaft and heard her voice. She was stuck between floors, but they managed to get her out safely. When she finally returned to her office, the staff told her to call your best friend because she would not stop calling. My phone rang; it was her. I cried for her and with her. I simply knew that she had been in trouble.

Now fast forward to December 17, 2018 and she's not answering her cell phone, and her husband is not responding. I decided not to think the worst. I convinced myself that maybe I was overreacting and to stop thinking so negatively. I said my prayers and tried to sleep, but it was a very uneasy night for me. The next morning, I called her cell phone and her husband's. This time her husband answered and told me that her limbs were very inflamed, she was lethargic, and was not making any sense. She had fallen on the bathroom floor because she couldn't control her balance or her limbs and was now being taken to the hospital by ambulance.

Afterwards, all she could recall was that she had been taken to the emergency room and heard conversations. Patty was asked questions but couldn't respond or partake in the conversations. It was all a blur. She could listen, but had no control over her limbs or voice.

Patty and I spent so much time there together. Her family and I were so perplexed by what was happening to her, that I rushed over to the hospital whenever I could, every day. I would sit by her side, talk and pray over her. She would sing church hymns: *Lord, Make Me an Instrument of Your Peace, Prayer of St. Francis,* continuously, followed by old disco songs like *In the Bush*, sung by Musique. I seriously did not know whether to laugh or cry. I couldn't understand what was happening to my friend, but I sensed she had internal bleeding.

Later, tests would show she had a large ulcer in her upper right abdomen. The tests would also conclude she had major kidney failure. Her family thought she wasn't taking care of herself, which upset me because I knew it wasn't true. When I was present with her, the doctor came in and said she had taken too many pain relievers, (which gave her kidney failure), she was malnourished, vitamin deficient, and suffering from severe anemia. It was what I call the illness thunderbolt, which I can say with certainty had been brought on by her mother's struggles with cancer, right up until the day she passed away. Apparently, the NSAID's high toxicity levels had traveled to her brain. My friend was placed under sedation, drifting in and out of consciousness. For two years, I had kept seeing something disturbing her brain, and thought it could be an aneurysm. Now it was all making sense. In my experience, spirit only supplies us with pieces on a need-to-know basis.

Patty had in-patient hospital dialysis three days a week, four hours a day. Finally on Dec 25th, a Christmas miracle, she finally became alert. Sitting by her side, I gently revealed that she had been unconscious for seven days and was now taking treatment for kidney failure. She then described her visitations from her deceased mother Anne and her father Charles, who were always sitting with her in a corner of the room.

Patty began slowly healing, and on January 4, 2019, she was discharged for rehabilitation until February 17, 2019, at which point her kidney function came back and dialysis ended. Throughout the following year, Patty was able to get about independently with a walker and cane.

On February 14, 2020 she went on an eleven-day Caribbean cruise, The cruise took place just as the Covid virus was starting in the United States. Luckily, she remained healthy throughout the cruise. The next day, after arriving home and while doing laundry from the cruise, she was walking with a laundry basket from the kitchen to the living room, when her left leg gave out and she went straight down almost like genuflecting. At that moment, she knew it wasn't like any of her previous falls. She tried getting help from her husband, but her leg was twisted like a pretzel. Unfortunately, it was so bad that her husband had to call an ambulance and she went back to the hospital.

There, it was determined that Patty had shattered her distal femur. She was taken into surgery where an external fixation device was put in place to stabilize her bones. This needed to remain until her bones became aligned, and a titanium rod surgically implanted. The fixation device was removed on March 17, 2020, with the rod and various screws being placed in her left leg and knee.

While waiting for this second surgery, Patty was placed in a local rehabilitation. In early March 2020, the Covid Pandemic was upon us, with the hospitals placing the overload of patients into nursing homes. At that time, all rehabilitation exercises and visitations were stopped, and patients had to remain in their rooms twenty-four hours a day. Patty's room was on the first floor and she had a bed by the window. That was the only way we could visit her.

My son, Michael and I hatched a plan to cheer her up. We printed out a sign with a picture of our first family cruise together to Bermuda from 2003. It read, "WE LOVE YOU - WE MISS YOU - GET WELL SOON!" We were on a mission and we headed for the rehabilitation center. Michael put himself between the window and a big thorny bush just so that he could tape the message onto her window. He knocked on the window. She became very emotional. We called her from our cell phone, and you could hear the joy and gratitude in her voice telling us that we had made her day for days to come. She explained to us later on that, as time passed, that picture kept her smiling for days until the one day the wind pulled it off her window. Patty was so touched by Michael's thoughtfulness.

She was given blood thinners, which helped dissipate the clots, and then quarantined in the hospital for ten days. It was April 2020, and at this point, she still needed rehabilitation for her shattered femur. It was decided that she be moved into another rehabilitation center that provided dialysis, physical therapy, and occupational therapies. Covid had now permanently damaged her kidneys.

She began dialysis and was given the therapies every day except on weekends. At this time, we were still on lockdown, so no visiting was allowed. As her best friend, I was crushed by these rules. She needed my support, and I was only able to do this by video call or via telephone. On weekends, her husband would drop off a goodie box with water and snacks. He wasn't able to visit on weekdays, but he never missed a Sunday and never missed including her favorite dessert - rainbow cookies. She stayed at the rehab until mid-August. She was alone on the holidays, which made me feel so sad for her, but I knew I could not feel as sad as she felt for herself.

Her husband and I would have conversations with her about what was happening in the outside world: what shopping was like at the supermarkets, Home Depot or any store for that matter…how we had to follow arrows on the floor, mandatory masking and stand five feet apart. She couldn't believe the craziness! Patty thought it was the most outrageous thing she had ever heard. She couldn't imagine it being this way in America. She eventually accepted that life could not be as she remembered it, and that this would be the new normal for a while.

The summer was over, she received rehab, didn't need dialysis, and she was finally coming home. She needed to use the walker to walk. Unfortunately, because of her inability to walk independently, she often stayed home, and because of Covid, she feared becoming ill and ending up in the hospital again.

She spent a quiet Thanksgiving with her husband, but for Christmas, they held a brunch at the house with all the windows open. There were no hugs or kisses, just fist bumps. It felt strange, but considering the previous holiday, when she was isolated in either the hospital or rehab, this year felt so much more hopeful.

The holidays passed, and it was now January of 2021. My friend's broken leg started leaking somehow. There was a little pin hole that formed where her leg had been stitched up and it had become infected. There were stitches from the top of her outer thigh all the way down to her knee. Who knew that this little pin hole would be the cause of another trip to the emergency room?

This time the metal rod had become infected, and she tested positive for sepsis. The surgical team told her she needed to have emergency surgery to remove all the metal, but they would not be able to confirm if they were going to be able to save her leg. I could hear in her voice her panic, but all we could do was pray for the best possible outcome.

After the surgery and she was in recovery from the anesthesia, she remembered asking the nurse if they had saved her leg. Yes!! They had removed all of the metal, except for one screw, which was keeping the thigh bone connected to her knee. Patty had been in the operating room for five hours. She was happy that the surgeon had been able to save her leg but was upset that her husband sat at home waiting to hear if she was ok. She knew that the worst-case scenarios were running through his head.

My friend was heading back to rehab again for more physical therapy. This meant starting off slowly, then increasing the times, days and the modalities, which would be intense. My friend never complained. She did what she had to do, and she was determined to live and get her life back regardless of what had happened to her. She has yet to get full steady use of her leg, but through perseverance and dedication, and with the help of a walker, along with individualized professional and personal support, she self-manages her dialysis, physical therapy, all necessary appointments and daily activities.

Currently, she is training and studying for home dialysis, which is not an easy task whatsoever. The dialysis center is very particular to those who are interested in taking on this endeavor. There are vigorous observations and training with someone you trust to help and support you at home. She is also waiting to be put on the list as a kidney recipient.

I wrote this chapter on an emotional roller coaster. At the end of it, I would just like to mention that with all that Patty has endured, she never gave up hope. She prays and has an enormous amount of faith in God. She is unstoppable, unbreakable, determined, a leader, super intelligent, loving, wise, generous, and strong. That's the short list. She is my soul-sister, confidant, …and a significant member of my soul tribe family. Your soul tribe, or soul family, is a group of people with whom you intuitively connect on a deep level. Soul tribe relationships are anything but shallow. There's a deep resonance at a soul level, which you intuitively understand is different and special.[ii] We don't have to verbalize our thoughts - we just know deep down what one another needs and have a very strong telepathic union. She is and forever will be "my person". God knew what he was doing when he blessed me with our friendship and I am forever grateful.

<u>UPDATE</u>

Patty is currently receiving dialysis at home with the assistance of a private aide. It pains me to add the sad news that on April 20, 2023, Patty's husband and our close friend Anthony, unexpectedly passed away surrounded by his close family.

Chapter 5
"Anthony Teaches Adaptive Gym Class"
This is Huge!

September 15, 2016: It was back to school night at the Center for Developmental Disabilities. I always looked forward to meeting Anthony's new teacher and hearing about his classmates, friends, and future goals.

The year ahead for Anthony sounded very exciting. He is a very social young man and he was maturing into himself. So much to look forward to. The gym teacher stopped by our meeting in the classroom and said, "you should be very proud of your son". I asked, "Why?" He replied, "Anthony is co-teaching and instructing adaptive gym techniques to the younger children". An adaptive gym class is made available to students with delays in the gross motor areas such as endurance, coordination, movement, and muscle strength. I asked the gym teacher to please repeat himself. Well, he did just that, and I was beyond and over the moon. He observed Anthony from the back of the gymnasium. He took over immediately and needed no direction. The boy that was mentored and supported by so many wonderful role models was now becoming a role model himself.

Anthony lives upstairs from where he schools. I called the residence and asked him to please come downstairs so that we could speak face-to-face and I could tell him how super proud I was of him.

He came downstairs with a huge smile on his face, and I pushed him for a hug and a kiss. He has difficulty showing affection at times because of his autism. We sat down in the family room and I asked, "Do you have any exciting news to share with me?" He looked at me and said, "I'm not sure what you're talking about". I replied, "What happened in gym class with the younger kids?" He said, "Oh that!" He looked at me and said, "I taught adaptive gym class to the younger children". I told him the gym teacher had shared the wonderful news with me. I asked, "How was it?" He said, "The children all have different needs, so I had to help them individually". I couldn't believe how he was able to articulate what took place in the gym. He expressed how some children needed direction in throwing, catching, and kicking balls, some needed help with running, jumping and skipping. I listened to him so intently. I couldn't believe that this was my son and his achievements.

On my way to CDD that evening, I picked up a Dunkin Donuts iced coffee and a few of his favorite donuts. After hearing such awesome news, I immediately rewarded him and we celebrated in the moment. His eyes were so bright and his smile was so big. He was proud of himself and I was so very proud of him.

I asked what he found to be most difficult. He said although he enjoyed teaching and being with the children, some needed more direction than others and at times weren't so cooperative. Also, at the end of class he had to direct them to pick up after themselves and put the equipment away. They did not want to participate at all. He explained how he had become frustrated with them, but then remembered he didn't like that part of gym class either in the past. LOL! He also expressed how he really liked supporting and helping the children. He could recall looking back when he needed support in his younger years and now how it was his turn to help them. He was paying it forward, as I like to call it. It was a very huge parental moment for me and my husband. Anthony's face glowed with pride as he expressed his emotions and experience. All I kept thinking was how far he had come and that our sacrifices were worth hearing about moments like this.

In the following few weeks, on October 16th, Anthony was going to be 18 years old. Please don't give up hope or faith. All things are possible. He is seizure free, verbal, athletic, non-behavioral and a typical teenager who wants to give service to younger children with special needs. Yes, he is developmentally delayed, but delayed doesn't mean NEVER. I'd like to think of it as a comma, not a period.

Hope is always there, even if we can't see it. Optimistic expectations can help change a negative situation into a positive one. Hope is "an optimistic state of mind that is based on an expectation of positive outcomes with respect to events and circumstances in one's life or the world at large." As a verb, its definitions include: "expect with confidence" and second "to cherish a desire with anticipation."

Chapter 6
"Guardianship for Anthony in Family Court"
Michael Has a Request

October 16, 2016: Anthony was going to be 18 years old. Eighteen is such an overwhelming age to think about for all parents, but especially those of us with special needs children. We now needed to file for guardianship of him. Guardianship is the position of being legally responsible for the care of someone who is unable to manage their own affairs, such as medical decisions and finances. Most special needs parents need to prepare ahead for this critical step because it could be an extremely stressful and emotional process, as well as a costly one.

I did some research and decided to take the task on myself to see if and what I could accomplish on my own. I needed to fill out and file a Guardianship 17A Petition, and I found an excellent tutorial online. Before I was seated, I gathered all the documents needed. As you listened to the tutorial, you were given ample time to fill out the petition as you went along online. I remember taking my time, spending two days to proofread and confirm that all the details were accurate.

After I had filled out the paperwork, I needed to hire an attorney to represent us. I turned to Danielle Brooks, my advocate and friend from Special Kids Advocacy Agency, for advice. She told me to look into the Hofstra Incubator. Depending on your financial status, they provide you with a legal intern and attorney for family court either for pro bono or a relatively small fee. I called the Hofstra University Incubator, spoke with an intern, and made an appointment for the following Thursday afternoon. She provided me with a list of questions that needed to be answered before the meeting and a request for legal documents including the Guardianship 17A petition.

Before even meeting with the intern and staff, my husband and I had a serious discussion on whom Anthony's guardians should be if something were to happen to us. (Another difficult choice that no special needs parent wants to think about.) We decided it would be Anthony's godmother Donna and her younger sister Amanda. It was an easy, yet hard decision to make. They were both special needs teachers and very good at their jobs. It wasn't about who could financially take care of him, but rather who would actually take the time to make the right decisions for him that he couldn't necessarily make for himself. They were both very loving, compassionate, supportive, and decisive. I could clearly see them working together as a team to get what he needed done. They would put him and his needs first. I asked them, and they accepted.

The following week, we met with an intern. She was professional, intelligent, informative, friendly and direct. She asked numerous questions and looked over all the legal documents and paperwork. She also explained in detail, that because of our income, we would be expected to pay a fee. The amount was not much compared to what other lawyers charged. I had made certain that most of the work was already done. Now the information needed to be typed into a court petition along with other court documents, proofed, signed by us, witnessed, submitted, and then we were to wait for a court date. If it were only that easy.

Two weeks later, I received a phone call that will be forever engraved in my memory. When we were in the meeting, the intern had asked, "Do either of you have a criminal record? If they were to do a background check, would they find anything on either one of you?" Of course, my husband and I both responded, "No." Well, they performed a background check - an incident that had occurred involving my husband when our son was five, which had been reported by his school, had come up in their search. It was declared unfounded by Child Protective Services after a home visit and a visit to their schools. Now, because of this technicality, we needed to add an amendment. This took a little more time, but this incident shows clearly why you need legal advice during this process.

After a few weeks, we were given a court date: September 29, 2016. My husband and I were to be in the Mineola Family Courthouse with Anthony at 9:00 am, with proceedings to begin at 10:00 am. We had spoken to him on many occasions about guardianship and what it meant. He is developmentally delayed, but he understood exactly why we were petitioning the courts to become his legal guardians now. He understood he needed our help with making medical and financial decisions.

Our attorney arrived to represent us around 9:30 am and we entered the courtroom at 10:00 am. The judge called us and our attorney to the front of the room. She looked at Anthony and said, "I've been watching you since I walked in, and you are a very well-mannered young man." My heart was full, and my eyes began to well up. She then asked, "Anthony, where do you live?" He responded in a clear voice, "At the Center for Developmental Disabilities and on the weekends with my parents." She asked, "Do you like it where you live?" He responded, "Yes, I have a great life. I have two families and homes that love and care for me." She said, "So lovely to hear you say that. Do you know why you are here?" He responded with a firm, "Yes! I need help making decisions for my money and health." She told him that he was very well adjusted to his life and added that we should be extremely proud of ourselves and our accomplishments as parents. "Your guardianship has been granted. The best of luck to all of you."

I was hysterically crying as we pushed the courtroom doors open. My husband asked, "Why are you crying?" Anthony replied, "Mom is happy." I was so relieved it was over and yes, proud of our accomplishments with our son. We were making so much progress as a family and it showed. All of our tears and struggles... and now, suddenly our son is 18 years old.

On the drive home, I realized how this experience was very different from the first experience in family court with my brother and parents. In our first court appearance, I had felt heartbroken, misunderstood and sad because my family couldn't understand that Anthony needed more help than what my husband and I could provide for him. Fast forward eleven years, and I felt the complete opposite - extremely proud of our decisions and of Anthony.

We asked Anthony where he wanted to go and celebrate. He explained that he wanted to wait for Michael to come home from school so we could celebrate with him so that was exactly what we did.

As we were eating our celebratory ice cream sundaes, Michael asked, "How difficult is it to change guardianship for someone?" I asked him, "Why?" He said, "I'm his only brother and I feel I'm supposed to help him make decisions for him some day." I swallowed so hard that my ice cream became stuck on the large lump in my throat. I told him that it was a very big deal and something for him to really think about when he gets older. He told us that he would be calling my cousin and letting her know that he would like to be his guardian in the future and asking her if that would be ok. True to his word, Michael had that conversation with my cousin. She reassured me that he sounded very determined – a lot like his mother! She told him that she was proud that he wanted to be guardian for his brother, but that he should wait because it is a big responsibility.

At the end of this chapter, I reflect on the relationship my sons have. Every parent wants this for their children. I've prayed many nights for them to grow closer and my petitions in both the spiritual realm and family court were granted.

[i] www.mayoclinic.com
[ii] www.dailydish.com

Chapter 7
"Grandma Angela Falls"
Anthony Calls 911 for Help

It was Saturday February 28, 2017: Anthony Jr. had asked if he could call Grandma Angela to invite her to his school for his spring show at The Center for Developmental Disabilities. He had dialed her number, and I could clearly see from the pale concerned look on his face that something was not right. He handed me the phone and said, "I heard a very loud crash. It sounded like Grandma slipped on the floor and was not responding. Grandma is hurt and Grandpa can't wake her up. I think she hit her head. Please Mom, hurry up and call 911 - she needs an ambulance. I think it's called a concussion."

As I listened, I could hear my dad trying to wake her. I had an overwhelming feeling I couldn't describe in the pit of my stomach (solar plexus). Solar plexus is a complex of ganglia and radiating nerves of the sympathetic system at the pit of the stomach in front of the aorta. "Celiac" comes from the Greek word for "belly" and "plexus" means "braid" in Latin. We call this region the solar plexus because the network (braid) of nerves looks like the rays of the sun.[i] My son grabbed his jacket and started rushing us out the door. I had called the ambulance before we left the house. The drive from Massapequa to Bethpage felt like it was taking forever. Time was in slow motion. I was so overwhelmed because we didn't know what we were going to find when we arrived.

When we pulled up the ambulance was parked in front, the front door of their house was open, and my mom was sitting up on a chair in the kitchen with an ashen face. I saw immediately that she had a huge bump on the back of her head, couldn't keep her eyes focused, and was having difficulty communicating. It was obvious that she had a bad concussion and needed to be taken to the nearest hospital for testing and observation.

They transported her to St. Joseph's Hospital on Hempstead Turnpike. We took my dad with us in the car and followed the ambulance to the emergency room. Anthony kept a very close eye on his Grandpa Armando to make sure he was ok. They put my mom in a private room off the emergency room. The head nurse came in and ordered MRI's and x-rays. I asked so many questions, advocating about pain medications and anti-nausea meds, that the head nurse thought I had a medical background. I explained that the years of being a special needs mom had taught me how to research online and had prepared me for circumstances like this.

She needed to stay overnight to be monitored. My dad was so concerned for her that I don't think he slept at all that night. My son Anthony stayed with his grandpa because he was worried about him. Anthony called me from their home and asked if his grandma was going to be alright. I reassured him that she would be fine, and for him to say his prayers and go to sleep.

The next morning, I spoke with the doctor who said that she was being released later in the day. He said it was nothing short of a miracle. I picked her up with the release instructions: she was to take prescribed medications and remain in bed in the dark for at least six weeks. She slowly recovered, but she was never the same after that fall. Her memory and communication had become stagnant. This was only the beginning of many concerns.

My son Anthony knew exactly what to do and remained very calm under a surmountable amount of stress. He had an abundant amount of unconditional love for his grandparents. I broke down crying later on but held myself together for him. I'm very thankful for the outcome, but when looking back, I realized it could have turned out very differently. It showed me how life can change within seconds. I also learned a lesson to never underestimate Anthony because of his disabilities because, in his case, the correct meaning of the word impossible is "I'm Possible!"

[i] www.healthline.com

Chapter 8
"Michael Makes the Varsity Football Team"
Go Varsity Chiefs

Before trying out for varsity football, Michael played for the Mustangs, and then Massapequa Youth Football when he was younger until he was bullied. He became anxious and depressed, so he stopped. As his parents, we were extremely bothered by what had happened, but we knew he needed a break. His emotions were so overloaded that he couldn't focus or concentrate. He decided to go back and play in middle school for the Massapequa Chiefs, and at the same time, we realized his earlier diagnosis of ADHD was incorrect. He was now diagnosed with Asperger's Syndrome. This was the reason why he was so rigid, needed to follow rules constantly, misunderstood social clues, and would perseverate so often. Yet, after his first diagnosis, Michael began pursuing some of his passions, such as computers.

In July of 2016, Michael decided to build his own gaming personal computer system. He ordered all the parts separately and put them together: LED lights, processor, motherboard, ram, solid state drive, hard drive, graphics card and clear tower case. It took him more time to find the parts online than it did for him to build it! (Approximately four hours from start to finish to be exact.) When he plugged it in at first, it would not work. Instead of quitting in disgust, he chose to trouble-shoot, and discovered that the small battery on the motherboard was loose and then fixed it. We were so proud of him. This is his passion, and he continues to pursue these paths even now.

Fast forward to August of 2017: Massapequa Chiefs Michael was participating in *hell week football*. What is *hell week* in high school football? Also referred to as "two-a-days," it is the period of time when practices start at the beginning of the season. Typically, for most football teams, hell week starts sometime in August, when the heat and humidity can make already-grueling practices that much more exhausting and demanding. He had mentioned to me that his goal was to play football in high school. As his mom, I was concerned that his weight would definitely be a negative factor for him making the team. His lack of exercise, which seems to be an issue for many in this age of technology and video games, could also hold him back. However, putting all of that practicality aside, I told him to pursue what he wanted, which was to be on the varsity football team.

It was a steamy hot summer in 2017. Michael was nervous about making the team, and I was nervous for him. Every morning I would pray to his guardian angels and St. Michael to protect him on and off of the field. If he was to make the team, then it should be for his higher good. I would go to the park where they practiced, and I would observe from a distance. Let me tell you, it was so terribly hot and uncomfortable. Even under those circumstances, these young boys had to engage in the most rigorous drills. Although Michael was high spirited and determined, he didn't make the team that year to play on the field. Instead, the coach asked him to be the team videographer. Technology and football are Michael's passions, so it was highly appropriate for him to be chosen for that position.

He called to give me the exciting news. He was somewhat disappointed but would still be considered a part of the team and this satisfied him. Again, I was so proud of him. He would travel with the varsity team to local games. He would set up his equipment on the field at the end zone. We would watch him from the bleachers as he filmed the games with such seriousness and accuracy. After each game, he would return to his high school, edit where needed, and present it to his coach.

As a football family, we would prepare the team breakfast every Sunday at the high school where the boys would arrive after they had attended mass and before their game. The local diners, bagel stores and nearby establishments would prepare delicious foods and also give them generous donations. The parents organized tailgating parties and dinner after the games. Once a week, a family would volunteer to host a pasta party for the team at their home. The other families would bring additional foods, drinks, desserts, etc. One week, Michael asked my parents to host. They made four pounds of pasta, eight jars of homemade sauce, one hundred and fifty meatballs and countless trays of chicken cutlet parmesan. What an awesome core memory for Michael and his grandparents! They were thrilled to participate in something that meant so much to their youngest grandson. This is what life consists of…beautiful heartfelt memories.

I must admit that Michael and I were not accustomed to such camaraderie. We happily found that the team parents, although they took their sports seriously, were indeed kind and generous. That was obvious when I was in the hospital - and the team families couldn't do enough for us.

In the summer of 2018, after the junior football season, Michael decided to go on a strict diet as well as a vigorous exercise regimen. He would work out five days a week with the other football players, which is where he made close friends. These young men would push him to do his best and even assisted him with his diet. As a result, Michael lost fifty-five pounds, and learned all of the drills - but would this be enough for him to make the Chiefs' Varsity Football Team?

It was September and the first game. The team was in the locker room and the coach handed Michael his Chiefs' football jersey, which read, GAGLIANO, #79. It was official — he had made the team!! Michael came out on the field that day in full uniform…and what a surprise it was! I was so excited for him. He followed through, believed in himself, and made it happen. It was going to be a fantastic junior year.

We were soon preparing for homecoming, which was a totally new experience for us. The cheerleaders had baked cookies and made individual football posters of each player for display. They would then go to each home, place an individualized team sign on the property, and leave a container of baked goods along with their football poster on the porch. Talk about team spirit! These cheerleaders had tons of enthusiasm and were full of fire and positive energy. These activities were all leading up to the actual homecoming.

The official Homecoming Day was October 20, 2018. As the football moms, we all met at the Massapequa High School Football Field to decorate after the team breakfast. This involved a lot of team work too and was not at all easy. The field was huge, and I was thankful that these women were organized, creative, talented, and full of energy. They created a huge football helmet in blue and gold (the Chiefs' colors), which was placed at the entrance of the football field. The players would individually run underneath it onto the field as their names were called. Their individual posters were displayed on the fences surrounding the field. We had put streamers and balloons everywhere imaginable. Now that we were all set up, we had to go home, get ready, and be back in two hours. I have to admit it was exhausting.

We arrived a half an hour early because we wanted good seats. The bleachers would get crowded quickly, and finding parking would not be simple. My parents, cousin Donna, and my friend Sharon (whose son played in the band) had come with us. The energy on and off the field was electric. My husband and I wore Gagliano team t-shirts with our son's number 79 on the back. When the players were announced individually, their parents were greeted on the field by their son and handed flowers. It was a day to remember…another milestone and memory that I would always hold close to my heart.

The Chiefs' official awards dinner took place on November 28, 2018. The coach and staff spoke highly of Michael, commending his team spirit, commitment, positive attitude, and physical transformation. He looked so handsome, wearing a suit and his warm smile, surrounded by the athletic staff and his teammates. My husband and I sat quietly, taking it all in as we silently celebrated how far we had come as parents.

Michael continued playing that year, and we enthusiastically attended each and every game. It meant so much to Michael that my parents had come to all of the home games. He speaks of it often since my dad's passing.

He graduated Massapequa High School on June 22nd, 2019. He has his driver's license and attends Nassau Community College for Computer Technology and Repair as his journey continues.

What honestly sticks with me at the end of this chapter is that I didn't know if Michael would ever make the team. I never mentioned that possibility to him. I kept my secret to myself and prayed about it often. For the first year, I believe it was divine intervention that made him the team's videographer. This position is what prepared him to be on the team the following year. He observed the team through the lens from a distance and saw what it actually took. Then, when he officially made the team as the underdog, he remained grateful and full of pride.

One evening, after one of the pasta parties, he visited the football field. Under his breath, looking at the stars, he claimed his spot on the team through prayer and proclamation. He knew that if he wanted it badly enough, he needed to be committed to himself in order to be successful. That was exactly what he did!

In the fall of 2022, Michael received a text from his former coach, asking if he was interested in videotaping the Massapequa Varsity Football Team with a salary. At the present time, that is what he is doing – and enjoying every minute of it.

Chapter 9
"Takotsubo Cardiomyopathy" Broken Heart Syndrome is a Real Thing

November 2, 2017: My phone alarm went off, Jake my fur baby started barking to be let out, I gulped down my coffee, took my thyroid meds, showered, dressed, walked Jake, and prepared for a follow-up IEP (Individual Education Plan) meeting for Anthony at his agency in Woodbury. His teacher, her supervisor, my two advocates, and I were to discuss his reading progress. I had been undergoing an overload of anxiety. I grabbed my cell phone and called my friend Patty to discuss the situation. For years, we had been talking about these meetings continuously, but to no avail, as he continued to not show any progress or improvement. I am sure we can all agree that there is a level of exhaustion and frustration that goes with being a parent and advocate for our special needs children. My son has actually advocated for himself for years and had been expressing his desire to learn how to read.

It was our usual dog walk, once around the block, accompanied by a very meaningful conversation with my friend. She gave me words of encouragement and told me, "I know that you know what you know, but please remain calm and in control, even though we both know you're usually right." Intuitively, I knew that he wasn't getting the one-on-one services to support his reading - just as I knew they would use excuses and fabrications. During our close conversation though, I had a strange heaviness in my chest as I was walking and talking, and I felt unusually dehydrated. Honestly, I thought nothing of it at the time.

I showed up at the meeting a half an hour early, reviewed my notes, and waited in the family room until my friends/advocates arrived - Danielle Brooks, and Maria Licatta of the Special Kids Advocates Agency. These ladies had been advocating and supporting both my sons for about 20 years. They get the job done!

We entered the conference room where they had me sit in-between them, strategically, for emotional and mental back-up. The teacher sat across the table, with her supervisor sitting at the head. The teacher arrived with five spiral notebooks and handwritten notes. We began the meeting with her telling us that Anthony received one-on-one support and supervision with a special reading program when he's not behavioral. I had provided the Edmark Reading Tutorial CD for the school so my son could get the training he needed. Next, she mentioned he was able to recall and recognize sixty sight words, but the advocates and I knew she was not being at all truthful.

My response to her first misinformation was that when Anthony came home for the weekend, he always informed me that he never received supported private reading attention. One of the staff members had also confirmed Anthony's statement to me in confidence. That being the case, I asked her to give me both the list of the sixty sight words that he knew so well, and the reading program CD so that I could help him at home. I also asked for his daily behavior notes from the teacher and staff, since his behaviors had been cited as the obstacle to his reading sessions. Finally, I requested that Anthony come into this meeting to read the sight words in front of all of us.

In response, his teacher flung her spiral notebooks onto the boardroom table and began to tell me about her many degrees in special education, demanding to know my qualifications that would allow me to question her abilities as a teacher. She was having a major temper tantrum. She then glared at me straight in the face and screamed, "I don't have to answer you!" and exited the meeting. I had previously confided to the administration and staff that she did not seem emotionally stable or had enough experience to teach using tactile stimulation instead of reading from a textbook. These children cannot learn this way. I had observed her teaching methods several times, and concluded they were not effective. How could she teach disabled children with behavioral and emotional issues when she clearly had no control over herself? Here, she had just proven my point.

Danielle told the supervisor that this teacher needed to take a deep breath and calm down. She further questioned, "What is wrong with my client's request if Anthony is not receiving the services listed on his IEP? Please have one of your staff retrieve the CD and provide us with the sight words." The teacher's aide could not find the CD, which meant it had not been used because if it had, I am sure it would have been found. Then, we were told that, because of attention and behavior issues, (which was their excuse all the time,) he had been unable to sit long enough to use the program. Lies, lies and more lies! The Massapequa School District had visited a few times unannounced, and the school's claims had been denied through observation. Anthony had been well-behaved and emotionally stable. Moreover, whatever is listed on the IEP needs to be followed by the teacher, school and support staff. They were therefore being non-compliant. If your IEP team is unsuccessful or unresponsive, you should consider filing a complaint with the district's special education administrator. That much I know.

The Supervisor asked us to get ourselves together and discuss the situation calmly. By this time, I had removed myself from the room due to the escalating stress. I returned with a glass of water, tried to take a deep breath… and couldn't. I was sweaty, clammy, and felt an excruciating pain in the middle of my chest. I looked at everyone and said as calmly as possible, "This meeting will have to end. I'm having a heart attack." Danielle exclaimed that I had a gray ashen look - and to get one of the staff nurses immediately. My advocates turned their purses upside down, looking for baby aspirin. Both advocates have parents with medical backgrounds. Danielle quickly called her husband who is a paramedic. She described the situation and my symptoms, and he told her to call 911 without delay. The 911 dispatcher was called and placed on speaker. I could barely communicate because the pain was unbearable. I did manage to ask them to please cover the small window on the conference room door so my son and other children would not see what was happening.

The staff nurse entered, "Cathy, please try and breathe. I have to take your blood pressure and, whatever you do, don't look at the numbers." Of course, I didn't listen to her. The systolic blood pressure was 179 (normal is 120). The diastolic blood pressure was 117 (normal is 80.) This was not good. The nurse firmly assured me, "Cathy, you're not going anywhere. Your work here is not done. You have so much more to accomplish."

The room suddenly started to get noticeably brighter; my Uncle Frank, my dad's deceased brother, appeared to me in a vision. He had on a black and red checkered flannel shirt, denim jeans, and a yellow safety helmet. His presence gave me so much peace. He said the nurse was right and my work on earth was far from done. It was not my time. He disappeared as the paramedics entered the conference room with the stretcher. They gave me baby aspirin, and I vomited into the garbage pail. I then started feeling new symptoms - nausea and severe back pains. The paramedics secured me onto the stretcher, rolled me out of the building, and placed me into the ambulance. Danielle came into the ambulance with me and held my hand. She looked at me and said, "Well I didn't see this coming today. Now I can say, oh yeah, by the way, one of my clients had a heart attack in a special ed meeting. First time for everything!" I started laughing - "Have you no mercy? I'm in so much pain, the paramedic is trying to run tests on me, and the peanut gallery is making me laugh. Stop it! It really hurts."

They took me to the emergency room at Syosset Hospital as a critical care patient with chest pains. Danielle stayed by my side and Maria followed the ambulance by car. The nurse helped me put on a hospital gown and proceeded to explain that the hospital was not equipped for cardiac patients, but please try and remain calm. Seriously? My day just kept on getting better.

Now, I have had to relieve myself since leaving my son's school. So, I got up to go to the bathroom, and this male nurse grabbed me, "You're going back to bed and can't get up without permission. We just got your results from the ambulance and your Troponin levels are way too high." (Troponin is a group of proteins that help regulate the contractions of the heart and skeletal muscles.)[i] When high, it usually indicates a heart problem. The heart releases Troponin into the blood following an injury, such as a heart attack. Now I found myself back in bed… and the nurse slapped a Nitroglycerin Patch on me. Within minutes, I was dizzy, nauseous, with a horrible headache - and I still needed to urinate! Now I was really annoyed. Immediately, I was put on a heparin drip, sodium chloride, and equipped with an oxygen mask. Mind you, it was not even certain that I had had a heart attack, but they needed to take all precautionary measures. Irritable, scared and distraught, I reminded Danielle I still had to urinate. The nurse went to get me a bedpan. I looked at Danielle and said "No! Please take me to the bathroom - I'm not having it!" I took my oxygen mask off, Danielle instantly grabbed the IV pole, and we snuck off to the bathroom.

During all this excitement at the hospital, Danielle was trying to contact my husband to let him know the current circumstances, but he had had his phone on vibrate because he was at a labor union strike meeting in Queens and did not recognize Danielle's number. In the interim, Danielle contacted Patty to fill her in, and to please keep calling my husband Anthony. She also told her to call my mom, tell her the meeting was running late, and that I would call her later - as per my instructions. After numerous attempts, and a few hours later, Anthony finally responded to Patty via text, but due to his Attention Deficit Hyperactivity tendencies and lack of comprehension of the emergency at hand, he did not leave the meeting until it was over. Danielle and Patty clearly did not want me to know because they had assumed he would rush to my side. As per my instructions, Danielle asked Patty to inform my son Michael, her godson, with discretion so he would not panic. At the time, Michael was the end zone video cameraman for the Massapequa Chiefs, and on this particular day, he was on the field with the team for practice. By the time Patty had reached out to Michael, my husband had already called him to inform him that something had happened to me, and I was in the hospital. Michael was so distraught that one of his teammates had to drive him home. Patty and I were so angry at my husband because we knew what a sensitive, anxious and worried young man Michael could be, especially because of his Aspergers.

Danielle also got in touch with my cousin Donna, filling her in on all the details and letting her know my husband was not reachable. She immediately drove to the hospital, where Danielle reviewed my condition with her. My husband arrived soon after. Donna and Anthony came to see me in the emergency room. She turned to my husband and questioned, "Why could no one reach you? When Danielle finally did, why didn't you leave immediately and come directly to the hospital?" He responded, "I went to the union meeting with my friend Mark, and since he came with me, I was his ride home." Well, things got very loud and heated quickly. I had never seen or heard my cousin lose her temper the way she did. She went after him so badly that my blood pressure began escalating again, so the head nurse asked them to leave my side and take the argument elsewhere. Danielle also asked them to calm down because it was affecting my blood pressure and making a stressful situation even more stressful. She directed Anthony to find the nurse to fill out the necessary paperwork, and asked Donna to spend time with me. Danielle didn't leave my side until my situation had improved enough for her to leave, which was around 9:00 pm that evening.

At that point, the physician's assistant came to ask the usual health coverage questions. She then inquired if I had been under a lot of stress." What happened today that brought you here?" I explained that my husband was now on strike with his employer, after being a loyal employee for about thirty-five years, and there seemed to be no end in sight. I then added that I have two sons on the spectrum. Exasperated with what had been happening that day, I responded, "Do you think I have reason to be a little stressed? Please have my husband take care of the paperwork and proceed to ask him your questions."

It was getting late into the evening, and I noticed my mom had called my cell phone. I asked Danielle to gently break the news to her and my dad. My mom then informed my brothers. Immediately one of them called Syosset Hospital to speak with the head nurse who was taking care of me. She gave him the details of my condition, said they were still not sure if I had had a heart attack, and was unable to confirm if it was Takotsubo/Broken Heart Syndrome. She also informed him that there were no beds available at St. Francis Hospital. He became very upset that I had not been brought there in the first place. He had connections there, and he would get me transported the very next day even if it took him all night to make the necessary arrangements.

The hospital staff became very anxious about holding me there overnight because they were not experienced with critical cardiac care patients. They placed me in a room with 24-hour surveillance cameras and a strange screen monitor. I felt like I was being held captive in a weird sci-fi movie. I was hooked up to a heart monitor with electrodes, IV's and an annoying oxygen mask. All of a sudden I heard, "Hello, I am the nurse monitoring you this evening. May I please have your name and date of birth?" You would think they would have given me some kind of warning, considering I was there for a critical heart condition! I had nurses coming in and out of my room throughout the evening to check my vitals. You cannot sleep in the hospital. It was the longest night ever.

Well, I didn't sleep at all that night, to say the least. I prayed throughout most of it, asking God, Lord Jesus, Mother Mary, and all of my angels to give me the strength to push through this — to guide, love, and protect my family - to please intervene and guide my doctors and nurses so that I would receive the best quality of care. I had no choice but to assess my life and question everything that had led up to this point. What would my family do without me? I thought of my sons. How did this happen? Was it something that I did to myself? Had there been a better way to handle my stress? The only thing that helped ease my anxiety was that visit from my Uncle Frank at my son Anthony's school in the conference room. I had felt his presence strongly. If he said I wasn't going anywhere, and that my work was far from being done, then I knew and felt those words to be true. My higher self-kept telling me to give my worries to God, and so that's what I tried to do. I had to surrender all of my concerns to him.

It was 8:00 am the next day, and I could see the sunshine coming through the hospital window. There was a reflection of a rainbow on the wall in front me. No words could possibly describe the heaviness in my chest. I felt like an elephant was sitting on me. A nurse gave me my morning medications, asked how I was feeling, and told me I was being transferred to St. Francis Hospital as soon as they were informed that a bed was available. She also let me know that one of my brothers had kept calling to make sure I was indeed being transferred.

By 11:30 am, a nurse had come in to inform me that they had received the long-awaited phone call about an available bed at St. Francis Hospital. Clearly, it was not a case of what you know, but whom you know - according to her. Now we were just waiting for the ambulatory transport to take me there. It was definitely worth the wait. The two paramedics looked like something out of GQ Magazine. I may have had a heart problem, but zero problems with my eyes. Take me. Take me away. It had been a pleasant distraction for the time being.

We arrived at St. Francis Hospital. The paramedics transferred my paperwork, checked my identification, asked me a few questions, and brought me to my room. A staff member immediately let me know that I needed a catheterization procedure done, and that the cardiologist would be in to speak with me shortly. (Catheterization is a procedure commonly used to evaluate or treat certain types of disease in vessels of the heart and other parts of the body.)[ii]

Now that I was in the room, my mind began racing when I soon realized I was not alone. My new roommate pulled aside the curtain, "Hello, my name is Doreen." She had such a sweet, calming, positive energy about her. I was so grateful to share my space with such a lovely person. What I was going through was stressful enough.

The cardiologist entered the room and introduced himself. He was handsome and reputable. I had already Googled him after the staff mentioned his name. He also asked me if I was under a lot of stress. In a few words, I explained to him our family dynamics and the dramatic changes that had been happening. That question seemed to keep following me. He explained the procedure and assured me that we would have a clearer picture of my diagnosis afterwards.

The transporter arrived to take me to the procedure room. I remembered it as being freezing cold - and that I had goosebumps from head to toe. The anesthesiologist instructed me to start counting backwards from ten. I remember counting backwards, with the last number being four - and mumbling something to the cardiologist.

I woke up in the Post Anesthesia Care Unit. The cardiovascular nurse took my vitals and asked how I was feeling. Another nurse had joined us; her face looked very familiar. She had been in the procedure room. She asked what the last thing was that I remembered. I told her, "Not much really." She laughed and said I told my cardiologist that he was handsome and to please make sure my hair wouldn't fall out from the anesthesia because that had happened to me before. As she was telling me this, I saw that he was walking towards me! Can I please hide my face now under the covers?

He reported that I had no blockages and the procedure had gone well, but that I had something called Cardiomyopathy/Unspecified, Takotsubo Syndrome (also known as Broken Heart Syndrome,)[iii] and Ventricular Tachycardia. Cardiomyopathy makes it harder for the heart to pump blood to the rest of the body. In some cases, cardiomyopathy may lead to heart failure. Broken heart syndrome, also called stress-induced cardiomyopathy or takotsubo cardiomyopathy, can strike even if you're healthy. The name Takotsubo is derived from octopus traps that resemble the pot-like shape of the stricken heart. Ventricular tachycardia is a condition in which the lower chambers of the heart (ventricles) beat very quickly. It can also be brought on by emotional stressors. It usually occurs due to a problem with the heart's electrical impulses.[iv] After that explanation, he told me I would be visited by another cardiologist who specialized in cardiac implantable device procedures. *Had I just heard him correctly? Was I getting a consultation on a defibrillator implantation before my 50th birthday?*

Why yes, I was! In came the other cardiology specialist. He explained that my current condition had been brought on by a rush of adrenaline to my heart, triggered by too much stress. My heart muscle was weak, my lower chambers of the heart were beating very quickly, and my heart could stop beating at any time. I was given a few days to decide.

I prayed every day leading up to my surgery. In the interim, I called my husband and sons to gently share the news. They were all so concerned and worried for me. Our family dog Jake kept urinating all over the house because I wasn't home, which pushed my husband over the edge. I asked him to please have patience. I called Michael a few times to check in on him because he had taken a break from school due to his anxiety and concerns for my health. He confided in me that he and his brother would be screwed if something were to happen to me. That's not how he said it by the way. He emphasized that he loved his dad, but he would be useless without me. We were so fortunate that the Massapequa Chiefs football moms sent food to our home daily, as did our many friends and family. I was surrounded by beautiful flower arrangements in my hospital room and had received so many well wishes along with many visitors. In times like this, you realize who is really there for you. I was extremely grateful.

On November 7th, I woke up to my roommate Doreen's playing "Sweet Caroline" by Neil Diamond, which was one of my Uncle Frank's favorite songs. There it was… my sign from the heavens above. That was my confirmation. Everything was going to be alright. My St. Jude's defibrillator implantation was done in the afternoon that day. I have often wondered if I had made the right decision, but my sons' loss of their mother was something I could not even begin to contemplate.

The next day, I realized it was going to take quite some time to accept this foreign object in my body. We take so many things for granted as humans. Until something like this happens - and then you realize how precious life really is. I was very emotional and in a lot of pain. They had to cut into the thick muscle tissue to the left of my breast, and I was wrapped up in bandages. Honestly, I couldn't stop crying. The cardiovascular nurse came over to take my vitals, and then asked me if I was ok. I said, "I just really want to take a shower." She smiled and said, "Ok, no worries, I will assist you." She covered my bandages with plastic, took me down the hallway to the shower, and cared for me. I was so thankful for her kindness, understanding, and compassion. I felt so much better after the shower. Why? Water is connected to your emotions in the metaphysical world. As I showered, I was also washing and releasing my worries away while taking in my gratitude for a second chance at life. Didn't you ever wonder why taking a shower always made you feel better? You're physically and emotionally clearing out what no longer serves you.

I was released a few days later with instructions to follow. I was prescribed beta blockers, blood pressure medication, baby aspirin, and bed rest for three months to help heal my heart. When I would take Jake out for walks, the intake of cold air made it more difficult for me to breathe. Sometimes I didn't think I would be able to make it home. My days and weeks consisted of cardiac specialists, watching my diet, and resting. The regimen was a blueprint for emotional, spiritual, physical, and mental healing. I was also suffering from PTSD and anxiety issues, which are not uncommon in cardiac patients. I had dreams about dying for the longest time. This was a life-changing and traumatic experience.

It is also very important that you listen to your body. The first three months after my cardiomyopathy, I experienced shortness of breath. I couldn't imagine living with this on a daily basis. I had visits with my doctor and cardiologist on a few occasions. My cardiologist's office was down the hall from my doctor in the same building. My doctor had always been a good listener, who was also respectful, patient, and kind. Being a mom herself, she understood the daily stresses. She asked what I thought was going on with my health. I told her the only things that had changed were the medications. It was not a mental feeling of anxiety, but rather a physical response. I know the difference. She determined it was an allergic reaction to my beta blocker, Propranolol, with side effects that could include constricted bronchioles, shortness of breath, depression, and nightmares. I cannot begin to stress enough how important it is that you become your own medical advocate and pay attention to how you feel. After a change in medication, I started to slowly work back to being myself.

At the end of this chapter, I leave you with this: I thought I had been doing all the right things to be healthy. I lost 120 pounds with bariatric surgery, watched what I ate, meditated, and destressed the best way I could. I never would have thought that I would become a cardiac patient. That day was like any other day, except I had had enough of one person's nonsense, for which I paid a very heavy price. As you can see, I have zero patience for dishonesty. So, my advice to all of you is that holding in stress will eventually kill you. Tell people off when necessary because some people need to be jolted into reality. Statistics show that most women cannot survive this trauma because they tend to ignore their symptoms. If I had been at home, I probably would have taken two Advil and gone to sleep. We all know how that would have turned out. Please be grateful for your family and friends. Always find a way to spend time with people that you love. Make sure you let them know how much they mean to you. Tell them *I love you*... Wake up every day with a grateful heart. Make yourself a priority because no one else will. If you don't, the Universe will make sure that you do.

My advocates soon took matters into their own hands regarding my son's education. Danielle and Maria explained that I needed to take care of myself. Their concern is something that I will never forget. The teacher is no longer teaching at the agency. She was replaced by a more experienced one with a tactile style of teaching, which is proven to be more effective with children with different processing and communication delays. She and her staff gave each child individual learning and reading time slotted throughout the day. I was in her classroom on numerous occasions, and the children were always smiling and learning. She had an understanding of the needs of the children as individuals. She was very compassionate, patient, and understanding. Through the years, I have come to the conclusion that most teachers are in that field for love, not money.

I will always celebrate November 2nd as my heart day - much like a second birthday. The following January 7th was my 50th birthday. I spent it quietly with family and friends. All that mattered was that I was still here! Perception is everything. Don't let anyone convince you any differently.

[i]www.medicalnewstoday.com
[ii]www.mayoclinic.org
[iii]www.britishheartfoundation.org
[iv] **www.mayoclinic.org**

Chapter 10
"Anthony Meets His Idol"
Wonder Woman, Gal Gadot

December 6, 2017: It had been a little over a month that I was in St. Francis Hospital with my heart issues. I was having difficulties with shortness of breath, but I was determined to push myself forward. During my morning ritual of saying my prayers of gratitude, saging, clearing energy, sitting and having a cup of coffee, my phone pinged with a text message from Joseph Allocco, our son Anthony's best friend's father. Joe is a generous kid at heart… one of my son's favorite people. He is a Disney, Comic Con, Avengers, Justice League movie enthusiast, and a collector of everything.   He has an impressive treasure trove of autographs, memorabilia, signed photos, etc. He receives updates on what's happening in our local area that our boys may enjoy, especially actors and actresses in adventure/fantasy films. He shares this hobby with his son Joseph and has always included my son in the activities. Can you see why he is so loved and admired by us? I have always felt a celestial peace in all things when collaborating with Joe and his wife Linda.

The text message read, "Cathy, this weekend December 7th, 8th, 9th, and 10th at the Nassau Coliseum, Wonder Woman (Gal Gadot) will be there along with most of the Justice League! It's the Ace Comic Con Long Island at NYCB Live!! This is a once-in-a-lifetime opportunity for Anthony to finally meet his idol, Wonder Woman. Her autograph is $175 and it's selling out quickly. If you're interested, we need to make a reservation, and devise a plan quickly." It was already the 6th, so that didn't give us much time, but if anyone could make a miracle happen, it would be Joe Allocco.

I went online immediately and read that the autograph purchase did not include a meet and greet. The $175 was just for her autographed picture. Ugh! I paid separately for admission tickets, which were $150 for three tickets. These were for my husband, Anthony, and me. The autographed picture was an additional $175. Now to break the news to my hardworking husband, who was recently on strike against Spectrum/Time Warner - where he had been employed for thirty-five years. He never hesitated, "Cathy, hurry up and put it on a credit card. This experience is going to be priceless for all of us!" What a man!! What a dad!! My husband knew how much it would mean to our son. As always, he and I shared the same souls. So, I did just that - put it on a credit card, and we would be off to the Nassau Coliseum that Saturday, January 9th. We then discussed surprising Anthony because he would perseverate until we would actually leave. With Anthony's Pervasive Developmental Disorder/Autism, it was important to keep it to ourselves at first to see how it played out. We really wanted both boys to meet her.

It was the longest couple of days. Joe and I reached out to Gal Gadot through all social media outlets: Facebook, Instagram, Twitter, her fan club, etc., but we never received a response, but that wasn't going to stop us on our quest. I kept praying for my angels and Universe to intervene on our behalf to have the boys meet her. They were such wonderful young men, and they deserved this fantastic opportunity. I would persist in picturing both of them in my mind's eye, standing next to her and smiling, while camera flashes surrounded them.

My son Anthony was obsessed with her intelligence and beauty. He would say, "Ma, she has beauty and brains." He knew every detail about his idol. Posters and life-size cardboard images of her embellished his room, she was on his phone's screen saver, and her image appeared on every shirt, book and comic book of his. He was a collector of Gal Gadot everything! He would constantly dream about the day he had the opportunity to meet her. What he would say to her… He should only know that his dream was so close at hand.

Wonder Woman Day had finally arrived! My husband and I woke up knowing we had a full day ahead of us. We told Anthony that morning that he quickly needed to take a shower because we had a special day ahead of us. My husband helped him shave and told him to wear his best Gal Gadot shirt. We briefly explained we had a surprise for him.

We drove to the Nassau Coliseum with hearts beating in nervous anticipation. Anthony had no idea until we pulled up. There it was - a tremendous banner placed front and center of the Coliseum that practically screamed, "LIVE! Henry Cavill, Superman and Gal Gadot, Wonder Woman!" Anthony's expression was indeed priceless. "Are we here for her?" No way?! I can't wait to tell Joe and his dad!" Mind you, he didn't even know the Alloccos were meeting us there in the lobby.

Upon entering the Coliseum, we saw them standing right in front, behind the red velvet ropes. Anthony and Joseph high-fived each other, beaming from head to toe. Joe Allocco announced in a serious tone, "We are going to try our best to make this happen." I answered with determination, "We will make this happen!"

We started our plan by approaching the concierge at the front, explaining that our sons had disabilities and that it would mean the world to them to meet their idol, Gal Gadot. We added the fact that we had pre purchased a signed autograph of her online. He explained that we needed to work our way to where the event was taking place, and if we could manage to make our way to the head of the crowd, there was a possibility of meeting her. The Justice League should be arriving shortly: Jason Momoa/Aquaman, Gal Gadot/ Wonder Woman, Ezra Miller/The Flash, Ray Fisher/Cyborg and Ciaran Hinds/Steppenwolf.

Since he was so familiar with Nassau Coliseum, Joe strongly declared, "We got this!" Linda backed him up, "If he said we got this, then we do!" We could see the floor set-up from a few levels above. You could just envision Joe's wheels turning. He had been to the Coliseum for so many concerts and meet-and-greets that he knew the ins and outs of this gigantic facility. A close friend of his coordinated the Eternal Con and other conventions, so he knew the set up. He lowered his voice and told us, "Follow me and don't ask any questions."

We approached these big doors, which were the entry to the underground tunnel between the Coliseum and the Marriot Hotel used by celebrities and bands who are performing. Joe said it was a longshot, but worth the try. He had an old lanyard around his neck, hoping no one would look too closely at it. Just to let you know, there was a sign posted at the front, which clearly stated "Coliseum Personnel Only or Those with Assigned Passes." Joe opened the door, repeating, "Follow me, don't ask any questions, keep walking straight, and don't make any eye contact. We just have to make it to the other side of the tunnel." That's exactly what we did! I should remind you that my heart was racing hard and fast. You would think that we were breaking the law. All I kept thinking was, "What we do for our kids! Could we get arrested for this?" Funny - but not funny.

We made it to the other side of the tunnel and through the doors. As we exited, we saw Nassau Coliseum Security ahead and then, as I turned, I beheld thousands of hardcore Justice League Fans behind us. The Coliseum employees asked how we had made it to the front the way we did? I was speechless, and about to become even more so. A few feet away, coming through those same exact doors where we had just been, strode the Justice League. We were front and center as they made their entrance. I was standing next to this massive 6'4" handsome man with long hair as my son hollered, "Aquaman, Jason Mamoa!" Behind him was Superman, (Henry Cavill), followed by a stunning brunette, in a red suit with red lipstick and a gorgeous smile…the one and only Gal Gadot/Wonder Woman. They all were walking to their assigned tents for photographs and one-on-one meet/ greets. Anthony couldn't breathe and turned very pale in the face. It happened within a matter of seconds. Talk about Divine Timing. I was at a loss for words. We had actually gotten that close to them without even knowing it.

Now we needed to figure out which employee could make our final dream destination come true. There were multiple lines, which were overwhelming -but we had made it this far. We had to keep going. We had one shot at this! There was a sign that read VIP's. Joe declared, "It's now or never!" The gentleman in charge of collecting tickets was very intimidating. When we explained our reasons for being there, he sternly informed us that the people there had paid at least $750 to $1,000 online to meet with the Justice League. Under his breath, Joe whispered if there was anything he could do. The man then asked, "Who's going in?" We replied, "Both boys for a meet and greet and signed autographs if possible." He was adamant that we should come back tomorrow because they were fully booked. Joe told him that "the boys lived in a group home" so that option would not be possible. He wondered if he could perhaps accommodate us while we were there. (Little white lie - my son lives in a group home, so it was a half-truth.) My husband then said the magic words: "Whatever it costs." We paid another $400 for both boys, he gave us all lanyards, and we placed them around our necks. He placed us squarely on the VIP line and said: "Don't make any eye contact, look ahead, don't answer any questions, and keep walking until you're under the tent." Familiar instructions!

We were on our way. Anthony was going to meet his idol and the girl of his dreams. The waiting seemed forever, but we knew that at the end of it, *she* would be on the other side of the tent curtain. The bouncer checked our bags, we walked ahead, and there she was, gorgeous as ever. She put her arms around both boys and said, "Smile, it was very nice meeting you both." Anthony had no words for her. He was absolutely star-struck. As a matter of fact, he remained speechless for most of the evening.

We did it!! That, my friends, is what you call Divine Intervention (the involvement (intervention) of a deity (divine) in the affairs of humans. In Christian religion, visions and miracles are often considered a form of divine intervention, with believers feeling they've appeared in the midst of a crisis or in response to prayers). When you say a prayer and put it out in the Universe, all the people and situations unite to make the impossible possible.

As we were leaving the Coliseum, it began to snow. We celebrated with dinner and ice cream at TGI Fridays. The boys were really stunned, especially Anthony. He walked around with her picture and kept looking at it. He said he was thrilled and exhausted at the same time.

After we had eaten, we went home, and Anthony went straight to bed. He told me that I was his Wonder Woman. He thanked us for making this unbelievable event happen for him. He said his heart was full because he got to meet his beautiful girl. He made his way downstairs to his bedroom. An hour later I went downstairs to check on him. He was sleeping soundly, with Gal Gadot's picture on his chest.

That night, before I went to bed, I thanked God and my angels for all the miraculous happenings of the day, and for sending us all of those helpful people on our path. If you believe, you can achieve! Nothing is impossible!

Chapter 11
"Tim Tebow's Night to Shine"
Anthony Goes to Prom With His BFF Joseph

January 9, 2018: I received a phone call from the Residential Supervisor at Anthony's agency, which my family and I will not soon forget. She called to tell us that Anthony and another student had been chosen by a nomination and lottery process to attend Tim Tebow's "Night to Shine" prom for children with special needs. It was going to be held on February 9th at 6:00 pm at The Bridge Church in Malverne. We were so excited for him to experience this very special milestone. For years we would watch students attend prom from Massapequa High School and, in my heart, I had always yearned for him to have the prom experience, a rite of passage for most young men and women.

Shortly after hearing the news, I called Anthony, who then explained that although he was very excited for himself, he didn't want to attend the prom without his BFF Joseph Allocco – who had been diagnosed with cerebral palsy, autism and epilepsy. He has a right hemiplegic due to a stroke he had at birth and his doctors didn't think he would ever survive. Anthony wanted to share this very special evening with him. He said, "Mom, I know if anyone can make this happen for us, it's you!" (Just a tiny bit of pressure!)

I had to do my research, send emails and make phone calls to make this happen for them. I also knew how much this would mean to Joseph's parents, and I wanted to surprise them with the news...that is, if I could make it happen. My son believes I am magical, so I had to try my best.

I said my usual prayers in the evening and morning and put the wheels in motion for manifestation. I would picture them in their tuxedos dancing in a huge ballroom surrounded by others smiling. I began asking my angels to intervene and guide me to meet all the right people to secure the best possible outcome for all involved. I felt strongly that if it was meant to be, the Universe would help me. First, I searched online to connect with the Tim Tebow Foundation, who put me in touch with the event coordinator, Dawn, of the Beacon Church in Nassau County, who promised to check if there was any room for Joseph to attend. This initial step took approximately two weeks of phone calls and emails, while patiently waiting to receive a final response. To our delight, Dawn called me back with a "Yes!"

The news was so wonderful that I was bursting at the seams to share it with the Alloccos. The family is well-known in Nassau County for their Franklin Square Horror House as well as their fundraisers for the autism community. It just so happened that we were having a get-together where they were to be in attendance, so I waited to tell them in person. I had mentioned on Facebook that Anthony received an invitation to attend the prom but had kept the specific details to myself. Although I was excited for us to attend, I didn't want anyone else to be upset who had not been invited. Such situations may cause pain to sensitive parents and children like ours, and I took it to heart.

When I met Linda, Joseph's mom, at the event, she asked how I was preparing Anthony for the big day. I then asked her, "If Joseph had the opportunity to attend, how would you feel about that?" She looked at me with a huge smile and said, "No way girl? You did not make that happen? You did not do this for us?" I laughingly responded, "Yes I did because I am really and truly magical!" Linda jumped up from her chair with tears in her eyes and said, "I love you and I'm so grateful to you!" I knew that I would cherish this moment for many years to come. To add more to the excitement, I informed her that, as parents, we were also invited to act as chaperones, and share in the special evening. She called her husband Joseph immediately, and he was just as elated as we were.

We only had only two weeks to order their tuxedos and make plans. I made an appointment with "Men's Wearhouse," and Anthony requested that my mom come with us so she could see him in his sharp looking tux. Anthony could be such a ham at times. The gentleman that measured him had the patience of a saint. He showed Anthony several different types of tuxedos - I was astonished at Anthony's fashion sense. He selected a perfect double-breasted black suit, a burgundy tie and handkerchief, and very outstanding shoes. The tuxedo was made to his exact measurements. We returned in a week to have him try it. WOW! Did he look handsome! There is really nothing like a sharp dressed man. ZZ Top's lyric just popped into my head, and I couldn't shake it.

On the night of the prom, we drove to his residence and helped him get into his snazzy new outfit. He wore a permanent smile on his face that would last all night. We took the requisite photos with the staff, and then left to meet Joseph and his parents at the Bridge Church. I had also received permission from the Foundation for Donna, Anthony's godmother, to attend. She is a special needs teacher who took professional pictures for all of us to remember "that night".

We all met outside of the Bridge Church where Anthony and Joseph were given their boutonnieres and met with their female escorts. They walked down the red-carpet arm-in-arm with their escorts, with music playing in the background, as they entered the Grand Ballroom. Sheer bliss washed over me as I watched the scene that I never believed would happen for him. Until this day just reminiscing about it makes me happy beyond description.

They had an incredible DJ along with huge Robotron screens for chosen speakers to communicate with the crowd. There were rooms where the girls could have their make-up applied and other rooms for the guests to play fun and exciting games. The boys were given limo rides in an area filled with loud music, colored changing strobe lights, disco balls, and singing with other guests. Anthony and Joseph danced together, with us, their escorts, and the other attendees. However, for as much as Anthony is charismatic and extremely social, he could be a little shy and timid if he doesn't know you. Here is where Joseph's personality comes into play. Not timid whatsoever, he is always dancing, talking, and on the move. It was very obvious to me why Anthony wanted to share this new experience with his good friend Joseph. If Joseph was there with him, Anthony knew he would feel more comfortable.

That night, Tim Tebow first addressed the guests - and then they all were crowned King and Queen of the evening. The food and desserts were a delicious assortment chosen specifically for them. They all returned home with an individual bag of souvenirs and pictures of their special night.

It was a prom to remember. We were all very impressed with the activities chosen for them, the organization, and all of the hands-on details. The excitement on their faces was unforgettable as they danced the night away. It was such an inspirational time for all of those involved. There are truly no words to describe how we, the parents, felt for both of them that fantastic evening. All things are possible with love, hope and faith! Don't ever give up. Sometimes hope and faith is all we have.

At the end of the evening, as we were walking to the car, Anthony said it all: "I'm exhausted, and I had the time of my life! I will never forget this moment! Thank you for making it so Joe was able to come." In my heart of hearts, I knew those few sentences would be etched in my memory forever. I am extremely grateful that these two young men were able to share an evening of unconditional love and acceptance - along with their peers. It is only just that they had such a water-shed moment that would change their lives for the better. They deserved it.

Chapter 12
"Soul's Journey Spiritual Retreat"
Healing and Transformation

June 1, 2018: In January of 2018, my spiritual teacher, healer and good friend Terry Lauria had mentioned that she was planning a *Soul's Journey Spiritual Retreat* with another teacher and acquaintance, Ana. I really thought nothing of it, but I couldn't say why. It had been eight months since I had had the frightening experience with my heart. Subconsciously, I felt nervous about being away from home, and I wasn't ready to step out of my comfort zone…especially for a week. It just seemed too long a time for my first venture.

A few months later, my mother's intuition told her that I needed to go. She and my dad sat me down in their kitchen and said, "Cathy you need to go on this retreat. Your father and I will pay for you to go. You need mental and emotional healing. You're just not yourself and you haven't been for quite some time." I had no idea what they were talking about. I wasn't able to see what they saw.

A week later, I went to visit Terry for our usual healing session. I told her that my parents felt that I needed to go on the retreat. I asked, "Where is the retreat being held?" She replied, "Massanutten Four Season Resort in West Virginia." I replied, "Are you kidding me?" For months on end, every time I would turn on the radio, the song, "Take Me Home, Country Roads" by John Denver would come on. I would hear him singing it in the car, in the shower, in my kitchen, with friends, with family, etc. I guess Spirit knew that I would be going before I did.

We were there for a little under a week, surrounded by beautiful mountains, wild animals, creeks, trees, etc. The setting was absolutely breathtaking. The condo was situated up high within the clouds. For a week, we would work on ourselves and experience intense healing on all different levels... mental, emotional and spiritual. In between sessions, we spent time at the resort for dining, taking ski lifts over the mountains into nature, and hiking trails. I met some strong, intense, powerful women. We shared a bond along with much laughter and tears. We were ladies from all different backgrounds, searching for deep healing and transformation in an open and safe environment. Some were divorced, or cancer survivors, or hospice administrators, or suffering from the death of loved ones. As an empath, the pain and suffering were unbearable at times. At orientation, just listening to their losses, I felt their heaviness in my chest. I empathize especially with those who had lost a parent, although I still had mine at the time. I excused myself at one point to return to the condo, draw a bubble bath, and call my parents to tell them how much I loved and appreciated them. That brief communication gave me solace and a bit of a respite from the pain.

At the end of every evening, I would video chat with my husband and Michael. I wore my glasses and no makeup because my contacts scratched my eyes, and makeup would just pour down my face from crying so much. I made my calls from outside the condo, and my husband would look so concerned. He would ask, "What are you doing there? You look awful! Like you're being tortured." I explained, "It's a spiritual retreat. We are healing and confronting our shadow side by dealing with emotions that we either don't confront, or don't realize we are holding onto." Of course, his response was, "You needed to go away to do that - and pay to be tortured?" Men! He continued, "You could have stayed home where I could torture you."

We also went on day trips as a group. We visited a beautiful farmer's market on a mountain, had lunch at a colonial tavern, and went to a local vineyard for a wine tasting and a delicious cheese board, followed by a delicious dinner. We found a beautiful lavender farm and learned to work with healing properties. Terry also brought us to the best-known restaurants for outstanding barbeques and cocktails.

I experienced Chi Kung for the first time. It involved performing movements that stimulate the flow of chi through the body. As such, it is often referred to as "meditation in motion."[i] Tai Chi is a system of Chi Kung that has been combined with the framework of a martial art. As such, it combines combat techniques with healing ones. I cried throughout the entire experience. I was releasing all the negativity from my chi and body. Chi is your life force = the energy that flows through you and through everything. It is that which gives us life. The concept of chi (also spelt Qi) has its roots in Traditional Chinese Medicine (TCM) and Martial Arts, but the belief in a vital life force energy and its role in our health can be found in many cultures.[ii]

We had Reiki Healing Attunements, which work by clearing energetic pathways in the body as a means of allowing Reiki energy to flow freely, particularly to areas in need of healing. Since attunement allows the student to connect with the source of universal energy, it can be a powerful spiritual experience. Reiki therapy is based on an Eastern belief that vital energy flows through your body. A Reiki practitioner uses gentle touch -- or places his/her hands just above your body - to help guide this energy in a way that promotes balance and healing.[iii]

Terry and Ana created each student's personal astrological chart. An astrology chart, also called a natal chart or birth chart, maps the planets in their journey around the Sun when you were born. It consists of your sun sign, moon sign and your rising sign. Your rising is your soul's purpose. I'm a Capricorn/Earth Sign (The Sea-Goat), Aries/Fire Sign (The Ram), Libra/Air Sign (The Scales), which are all cardinal signs. I thank God for the Capricorn in me because it keeps me grounded. Aries is the fire in me which gives me passion, a sense of warrior, and a duty to move forward. Unfortunately, my Aries moon means I have no patience, which is one of my life lessons. My Libra rising indicates that I need to find balance and fairness in this lifetime. These sessions helped me realize my soul's purpose is to help and guide children with disabilities, their parents, and caregivers. Our astrological chart also shows us our areas of transformation.

We also experienced a multitude of meditations from *Shamanistic Journeys for Healing*. One brought us cleansing through water and emotions. Fortunately, there was a specific moon meditation at the precise time we had a full moon in our line of vision, directly above the condo. We also did color therapy. Color therapy (or chromotherapy) is an alternative remedy that uses color and light to treat physical or mental health by balancing the body's energy centers, also known as chakras. This concept dates back to the ancient Egyptians who used sun-activated solarium rooms constructed with colored glass for therapeutic purposes. The colors are connected to the emotions and manifest where they may be stored in the body. We used our own intuition to get rid of the negative emotions. My negative emotion was black in color, identifying the fear attached to my heart disease. Once we had realized what this blackness was, Terry was able to replace that emotion with joy. I infectiously laughed for hours that evening, and everyone around me shared in my purely joyful Buddha energy. After that my jaw, mouth, and body hurt. I had peed my pants. I knew my going on this journey had been the right choice.

It was an experience I will never forget. I had no suspicion that I had been holding onto all this fear. In our everyday life routines we sometimes protect ourselves from what is really happening inside of us emotionally. Obviously, the emotion for me was fear - fear of my heart stopping. When it became time to release it, my body could not let go of it. The only way out was through my throat, and I would not let go of it. Eventually, with the help of one of the Reiki Healers, Aggie, and some spiritual tug-of-war, my fear was released on all levels. I ran to the bathroom to physically vomit, to expel it from my body. The process is very difficult to explain; it is something you would need to experience for yourself. Afterwards, I felt extremely light and at peace. Revelations that I had discussed with others uncovered emotions and feelings I didn't know I had been retaining deep down inside. This brief retreat culminated in intense growth and an all-encompassing sense of healing.

[i]www.healthline.com
[ii]www.nccih.gov
[iii]www.natureswayreiki.com

Chapter 13
"The Announcement of the Coronavirus"
How *Pokémon Go* Bonded Our Family

Week of March 9, 2020: Something I've been feeling intuitively and intensely was about to become a reality. For many years, I would have conversations with my mom and spiritual friends about a society that does not appreciate what they have in their lives. In the United States there is always a desire for more but never being wholly satisfied. It's a vicious cycle that continues because of TV ads and programming. The message is consistent - once you receive the next best thing, you will then be happy, which is not true. Status symbols come and go quickly and then it is on to the next *must-have* item in order to fill the void. Sometimes, working on yourself (even subconsciously) to attain self-awareness, is the greatest gift you can give to yourself, your children, and the generations that follow. We need to break that karmic dysfunction that exists in every family and learn the basic needs for our survival. This day was going to be the first day of the lessons we were about to learn.

I will backtrack two years to an astrology session with my spiritual advisor and teacher. We were seeking some answers because of the political angst in the world. There was going to be a financial crisis of some sort in the government affecting masses of people all over the world - as well as international banking. WHAT? I was thinking the stock market was going to crash. I could hear the seriousness in her voice, and I could read her energy since we had been close friends for many years. Whatever was coming, I was going to be prepared. Astrology does not lie. She looked at me and said, "Cathy we are being warned by Spirit that whatever is coming, you need to clear out your debt, and pay off your car loans! Budget yourself more carefully, especially since your husband has been out on strike."

That same evening, I sat down with my husband to have a serious conversation. I explained to him how I felt, and what we needed to do to prepare ourselves for what was coming. He looked at me and said, "Whatever it is you're feeling and thinking that we need to do, do it! I love you and you're usually very accurate with your gut feelings." Our thoughts were that if nothing happened, we would be in a better place than before. If something did happen, we would at least feel better about our financial future. So, we confidently proceeded with the plan, fully prepared to face whatever was barreling towards us.

On March 9th, my husband was watching NBC and heard the news anchor, Lestor Holt, announce that the Coronavirus (also known as Covid-19) had been detected in the United States and was spreading quickly. This was now officially a global pandemic. My husband looked at me and said, "This is what you've been feeling!" It was first reported on December 31, 2019 by the WHO (World Health Organization) as a pneumonia outbreak in Wuhan, China — a little over two months had passed and now it was given a new name - and Covid-19 was here.

Many past viruses had been contained; I was hoping this one would follow the same pattern. Well, I was very wrong. It was wishful thinking on my part. To save money, the political powers had dismantled the very policies put into place by previous administrations to protect us from situations like this... we the people were going to suffer the consequences for the current administration's short sightedness.

In March of 2020, a three-month lockdown was initiated. Most jobs and schooling were mandated to be done from home using computer videoing and technology. Masks were required wherever you went in public. First, it was the 2016 presidential election between Donald Trump and Hillary Clinton that divided our nation. Now it was going to be the global pandemic that he denied even existed, which would clearly divide our country and put our safety at risk. The news outlets broadcasted conflicting, flip-flopping information regarding the virus (depending upon their target audience), which made the public even more uneasy. No one could differentiate fact from fiction. Social media and the news were two of the biggest platforms splitting the country in two.

Looking back on that time. I believe that the pandemic's ultimate purpose was to show us the way back to basics and to teach us how to focus on what was important. We were confined to our homes, left to confront the shadow side of our lives...alone.

What is the "shadow" self? According to psychologists, the shadow self is the side of your personality that contains all the parts of yourself that you refuse to recognize, which is why we are oblivious of it. It is only through tremendous effort to develop self-awareness that we actually *see* our shadow selves. Although many believe the shadow self to be our negative side, this is not really true. The shadow self is actually what you yourself perceive as dark and weak about yourself, and therefore has to be hidden and denied.[i]

The pandemic forced us into spending more time on our relationships. There was now an abundance of time to be with your family or partner - to sit together at the table for family dinners, just talking. There were no distractions such as dance school, sports practices, music lessons, or anything to pull you away from spending time together. Pre-pandemic, you went to work to pay your bills to put food on your table, even though you may not have liked your job or felt under-appreciated there. Sometimes the people in your office were full of such drama, and now being at home, you felt relieved to be free of them. Other times, the opposite occurred – you realized that you were working beside such wonderful people, and you couldn't wait to return to work. The pandemic caused conflicting emotions, but that era served as a time for both reassessment and appreciation to determine that which we needed to either work on – or simply abandon.

Of course, there were considerable downsides to this virus. Hugging was frowned upon along with shaking hands. You couldn't see if people were smiling under the masks. I could read body movements and energy, and perceived that most people were cautious, terrified, and worried. In some eyes, the deep fear of what was going on was clearly evident. Children couldn't play together. Adults had to deal with children being home schooled on their computers, while also undergoing the stress of working from home. Physical meetings had ceased for quite some time, alienating all of us and impelling us to socialize in a different way. We were using FaceTime and other apps to stay in touch with family, friends and coworkers. However, as hard as these times were, we were much better off than past pandemic populations. Talk about stress, anxiety and depression! They had no way of knowing if their loved ones were dead or alive for a very long time.

More crucially, millions of people were losing their lives to this virus. This virus had no discrimination as to whose life it was going to take. I always try to remain in neutrality. (Neutrality is the quality or state of being neutral. It sets you free. It helps us see something more like the truth instead of experiencing circumstances in relation to expectations and desires, thus providing clarity.[ii]) At times, I strongly felt that some people were playing Russian Roulette with everyone's lives (ego), not caring about the well-being of others, or themselves. Ego is a person's sense of self-esteem or self-importance: the part of the mind that mediates between the conscious and the unconscious - and is responsible for reality testing and a sense of personal identity.[iii]

I personally didn't lose anyone to the Coronavirus, but I feel a genuine sorrow for those that had. My brother and his wife almost lost their lives to the deadly virus. His entire family had it. My eldest niece's parents were hospitalized with it. Her youngest sister was affected mentally by the virus, and needed outside help, which she received. I was, and still am, so proud of the way she handled her responsibilities as a young adult. We pulled together as a family, helping, supporting and loving one another. I would visit my parents to at least see them through their glass storm door and drop off needed supplies on their front steps. Then I would cry as I drove away. This situation began to change everyone mentally, emotionally, and physically. Mental illness skyrocketed since this virus was unleashed on us. Spiraling stress was leading to breakdowns of the body, mind, and spirit – everywhere.

We worried about our health and that of those around us. The stress and emotional upheavals were insurmountable. Moreover, anxiety over finances was infiltrating all of us, existing throughout the whole of society, rich and poor.

The most vulnerable were the elderly and the special needs community. The most fragile souls who lived in nursing homes lost their lives because of poor decision making. Visiting was limited or didn't exist. Some of the elderly most likely died from loneliness or the absence of their loved ones. The same rules applied for the special needs adults living in residences.

We missed our son Anthony terribly during the lockdown and pandemic, and so Michael came up with a creative idea to remain in touch. Anthony's X-box was at home with us so Michael purchased another with his own money, downloaded it with games, and got an X-box Live package with headphones so they could play and communicate every day. Michael then went to Anthony's residence to drop off the new X-box for his brother. This one idea was a game changer. (No pun intended.) It kept both my sons in communication with one another. Anthony could confide in Michael about what was bothering him and vice versa, which helped them both emotionally and mentally because now they had each other and were not alone. Their interaction helped since we were not going to be allowed to visit Anthony for quite some time. These pandemic protocols made no sense to us because the residence staff members were able to go home to their families, and then return to work with the special needs residents. The virus was constantly traveling back and forth, but there was only so much that could be done to keep as many people as possible safe. I appreciate everyone that took care of the most vulnerable, especially in the special needs community. I am very grateful for the staff and administration that sacrificed their time.

I would find my solace in praying, communicating with my spiritual friends and like-minded people. I would take long walks outside to immerse myself in nature. I began writing notes in my journal to express how I felt. I spent time with my neighbor Jill, creating crafts with her Cricut, and playing with her beautiful toddler, Mason, who always wore a smile that lit up a room. I call it the pure magic of innocence. This little boy is a natural born healer. You can clearly see how his infectious personality and socialization shower people with a positive light. I also spent time with my family, appreciating all that my husband and I had built together.

During this time, my son Anthony had moved into his first permanent residential placement, but it didn't work out. We moved him back home and were fortunate enough to have him with us by choice. Although at times it seemed difficult because his routine was not as regulated as before, we managed to make it work. Things always happen for a reason. There is so much truth to that statement. Michael had not had much time with his older brother because Anthony had lived outside of our home since the age of seven. Now, they were going to do some well needed bonding and catching up – living together as brothers again.

They truly bonded over Pokémon Go. The goal in Pokémon Go is to catch as many Pokémon as possible, then battle them at gyms. The key factor that makes this smartphone game different from past Pokémon titles is the way in which this concept is executed. In Pokémon Go, you move your character by walking around in the physical world. As a parent, I was thrilled to see how this game brought our family closer together, especially my sons. Michael downloaded the app on our family's cell phone, which gave us a reason to go outside in various parks and places together. We kept communicating about how we felt, and what was happening around us while playing. We would pack lunches and visit various parks and locations. Our phone would alert us as to what Pokémon we could catch, or battle against in our area or other areas. It was a blessing, and I was grateful for the chance to join together in a common goal… something that most people take for granted.

At the end of this chapter, I realized how people can get caught up in societal nonsense and lose sight of what's really important. Strengthening ties with family and friends is something you will never regret. Good health is your wealth. If you don't have that, you have nothing. I spend time and surround myself with quality people, not quantity. Always remain with those who clapped when you won - and those who sat by your side when your heart was hurting. That thought made me very aware of whose energy worked for me and whose I will no longer tolerate. This pandemic was an eye-opening experience that pushed people out of their comfort zones to evolve, made us feel uncomfortable, and tackle life-changing decisions.

[i]www.orionphilosophy.com
[ii]www.study.com
[iii] www.oxford.com

Chapter 14
"Anthony's Graduation From CDD"
Coronavirus and Uncertainties

In the summer of 2020, we were six months into the Coronavirus. All the years of sacrifices our family had made were coming to fruition this year. Anthony was finally going to graduate! We had long been looking forward to this moment - for what seemed like forever. We had always planned on throwing an unforgettable graduation party to celebrate all of his accomplishments. Now, Covid was forcing us to rethink those plans, but we still wanted to celebrate "HIM." He had worked so hard to reach this major moment in his life.

Anthony had been attending the Center for Developmental Disabilities and was scheduled to graduate at age twenty-one. NYS Education Law, Section 4402(5) indicates that students with disabilities reaching the age of twenty-one between July 1st and August 31st are eligible to remain in school until the 31st day of August or until the end of summer program, whichever occurs first.[i] As such, the journey is longer, challenging and more complex for special needs students and their parents. We just hope and pray that they have learned enough academics, socialization, and life skills to be successful in our society. We all worry about our children, but for special needs parents… we very much fear the future when we are no longer viable enough to advocate for them. What will happen when we are no longer here? That question is consistently in the mind of every special needs parent or guardian — and it never goes away.

Anthony was being schooled via Zoom and this method was challenging for many children with or without special needs. He would call or Face-time with us, often frustrated because he missed us, his family, his teacher, classmates, and most of all, his routine. This situation continued for the entire lock-down, and even a few weeks afterwards. I kept reminding him that he was safe, loved, being cared for, and that was all that mattered. Yet, once the session ended, I would become hysterical, and then repeated those same reassurances to myself. My heart was so heavy.

He kept in touch with his best friends Joseph and Brian. They would send each other packages, and communicate through Facetime, texts and phone calls. Then he would call me to share his excitement in finding out that his friends also missed him. We asked all of his aunts, uncles, cousins, and our friends to call him at his residence. The CDD Parents Association sent catered food, delicious desserts, projects, and special gifts to all the residents in lock-down. Anthony felt the love - that's all that mattered.

One day in June he called and said, "Mom, I was outside on the enclosed rooftop looking at the sun, trees and flowers. It was so beautiful, but I kept thinking in my head "how can there be a deadly virus in the air that we can't see or touch, but can make us sick and die?" Then he said, "We don't control any of it, God does!" He had heard me say this in the past, and now he was repeating my own words back to me!

The months of lock-down without him felt like a lifetime. He constantly asked if he was really going to graduate and have a party with his friends. There was so much confusion about the virus due to the differing announcements being made by the school district, governor and mayor's offices. We just needed to be patient, but how?

We received an email from our social worker to confirm that he was going to graduate with his friends on July 21st. Masks would be required, and seating was limited to four attendees. During the pandemic, my husband and I had already decided upon a surprise graduation party due to his nervous anticipation over not knowing. Then, if we had to cancel, he would not be disappointed.

We planned for the graduation surprise party to occur on July 12th, ten days before the actual ceremony. I shopped for the party supplies and hid everything in the garage. We had delicious Italian catering, and ordered a huge outdoor tent, table, chairs, and fans for plenty of ventilation. We also held the party outside - in front of our home - so we could keep a safe distance among the guests and tables. We hired a terrific DJ, Keith Ray from Stingray Entertainment. (Keith also has a special needs son, and is well known for his kindness and professionalism throughout the community.)

The big question remained: how were we going to pull this off with Anthony being home for the weekend? I asked Brian's mom if she could take Anthony for an overnight stay with Brian on that Saturday the 11th, so we could get prepared for his party. She agreed. Of course, on that Saturday, Anthony just wanted to come home, calling us a few times, but Brian's mom kept him busy and preoccupied. Knowing Anthony, this was definitely not easy!

On the day of the party, Anthony arrived at his long-awaited graduation party and became extremely emotional as well as surprised. We had pulled it off! We had invited his mentors, friends and his family so that he could celebrate with the people who had loved and supported him through the years.

As I planned the party, I worked to ensure the safety of my guests, taking such steps as providing hand sanitizer and alcohol wipes at all of the tables. If people decided not to come, it would be their personal choice. I prayed every day and heard the same message - everyone was going to be fine. My spiritual prayer warrior and friend Sharon arrived and helped with the decorations. We said prayers on the property and placed blessed rosaries from the Vatican in the above middle part of the tent. We set our spiritual intentions upon everyone attending the party to be protected from the virus and wished them good health for the future.

We had one decline from a close family member: my brother. We found out afterwards that they had had plans to be in Montauk with their friends. What I found to be most upsetting for me as his mother was that my son kept looking for them - and missed them. They never called to congratulate him and explain why they had not attended, or even acknowledged his achievements with a gift. He was simply ignored. This disappointment is etched in his mind and heart. I still hear the bewilderment in his voice to this day. They chose to be with their friends - not me. This was his uncle; someone he had always idolized. He looked to me for answers, but I had none to give.

I am happy to say that the party was a great time for all that attended. Anthony well deserved the recognition and accolades for what he had gained for himself through the years. He was moving forward - onto bigger and better things. It was such a wonderful day of celebration that for this one moment in time, the deadly virus had ceased to exist.

Graduation Day finally arrived. I remember waking up with severe sciatic nerve and hip pain. For those that don't know, anything related to the hips is connected to moving forward and, in my case, to all of the uncertainty over what the future was going to look like for our son and us as a family. There is also a correlation between your hips and the sacral chakra, which is associated with our ability to express emotions, experience pleasure, and enhance creativity. My emotions were all over the place. I was not vocalizing the conflicting thoughts running through my head about all of the tragedy and death swirling around us, juxtaposed against my own happiness and pride. As an empath, I work daily on having a positive thought process and outlook. (It was mind over matter.) To achieve this state, I surround myself with positive, uplifting, like-minded people.

This was to be Anthony's day. Regardless of my pain, I was sailing through it like I had so many times before. One of his favorite teachers had left during the pandemic for a better position. I was extremely happy for her. I thought the children would be happy to see her warm familiar face again, so I gave her the remaining ticket we had been given as a family. My son, other students, and parents were overjoyed by her presence there. She was a kind, loving, and compassionate teacher who truly cared about her students' progress. Every one of us recognized that, for her, the children always came first.

It was a wonderful ceremony, despite the virus. Although masks were required, and there was this deadly virus lurking, nothing could stop us from celebrating our inspirational children and the progress they had made. The students were announced individually, with speeches being given on behalf of each one of them. The administration, employees, and parents were beaming from ear to ear. We gathered as a group to take a final walk together around the entire perimeter of the building. The other students and staff stood and waved good-bye. It was a bittersweet moment and the end of an era.

Looking back on his graduation and party, I have no regrets. I've come to the conclusion that if we had not given the party back then, it probably would not have happened for a while. As a result, the excitement of the moment would have been lost. Another important lesson to be learned is that people and their patterns don't change. Some will continue to disappoint you. Remember - people eventually expose who they really are, so believe them when they do.

Sometimes you just have to keep on moving forward, reminding yourself that you are doing your best. Have faith - and eventually all will fall into place.

Chapter 15
"My Mother-in-Law Falls Down"
The Dreaded Phone Call

October 19, 2020: I woke up to the sun shining through our bedroom window. I was excited because I had plans to go hiking in Kings Park Bluff with ladies from my friend Susan's Goddess Circle. Susan is a healer, a medical intuitive massage therapist, and a magical singing bowls master. (Singing Bowl Meditations, also known as sound baths, are used to stimulate/calm brain waves, help lessen chronic pain, engender mental health, boost overall well-being and lift your vibration.) The entire process is what I like to call a spiritual massaging of the soul. It uplifts me to be in the company of such like-minded, spiritual, and highly attuned spirits.

The five of us gathered at Susan's home at 11:00 am, Susan, Coleen, Kim and Marie. We took Coleen's van since she had been there before and knew the route to King's Bluff and the trail. We packed water, snacks, cell phones, flutes, and a singing bowl. We were going to walk the trail to immerse ourselves in nature. It was a picture-perfect day.

Upon arrival, I looked at the time, and noted it was noon. Everyone's cell phone coverage was spotty, so it would be unlikely for anyone to reach us while we were in the park. There were many steps leading up to the trails, which most likely meant the elevation was going to be high. Did I tell you that I am afraid of heights? I would be facing one of my greatest fears, but I couldn't ask for better companions to be by my side.

We ascended the steps, spotting the trail, enormously beautiful trees, and finally the magnificent view. There were sand mountains as you approached the edge, and a vision of blue waters below. People were walking up and down the trails, enjoying the scenic views. Since we had just arrived, I suggested we should make our way down to the water later in the hike because it didn't look easy to climb back up again after working your way down.

We continued onto the trail, looking for specific marking symbols on the trees in order to correctly follow the path. As we proceeded to walk, the route became narrow and winding. Since many of the tree roots were protruding upwards, I had to find something to hold onto because, as I looked down, I could feel my stomach lurching into my throat. Moreover, I soon realized the markers on the trees were either very light or simply non- existent. We just kept going deeper along the trail across many different terrains. We had managed to hike up hills, over water, through thorny bushes, and onto entirely different trails altogether. We took our time, sharing stories of our families, spirituality, life experiences and wisdom. We confided in one another, and although we had walked for hours, we did not really notice the time passing because we were involved in our conversation. The fact that we did not know where we were was not our top priority.

Remarkably, every time we stopped and wondered about our location, we met someone who just appeared out of nowhere. I could not explain how we came across these helpful people. As we made our way, we stopped for water, played our instruments, hugged a few trees, and intoned our mantras that were mostly about self-love, gratitude and manifestation. We spoke of alignment. We repeated,

> *"I am attracting better because I discovered that it all starts with me. I am going to change myself first so that everything can align for me. I'm not going to blame anyone. I am going to take responsibility for my life. The better I become, the better I attract. There is a past version of myself that is so proud of how far I have come and continue to become."*

We discovered how the Universe works to align you with people, objects, and situations that match your energy output. As a group, we agreed that the more you improve yourself, the more you find people or activations that benefit you. The more you continue to have a grateful heart, the more blessings and abundance will freely enter your life. If you hold onto resentment or negative situations, you will block your abundance and blessings. It all needs to flow smoothly into your energetic field, and it all begins with you. You can be spiritual as well as heartbroken, depressed and angry. You can experience many emotions, but just feel them - and then let them go. Do not be defined by the emotion or remain stuck inside of it. That is when illness is created in the cellular tissues of the body. Spirituality helps you to face the Human experience, not suppress it.

As we forged ahead, we were told by a hiker to look for a fence, which bordered a very long path. He said to follow that path to the restrooms and parking lot. Well, that path was approximately three miles long, and it took us to the opposite side of Kings Park Bluff and trail, but at least we had made it to the restrooms (three hours later). We ran into a couple getting into their car, who told us to walk across the parking lot to get onto another trail that would take us back from where we came.

That is exactly what we did - and we followed that trail back for another hour. The hike back did not seem that bad because some of it seemed very familiar, and the markers on the trees were now more visible. Finally, we made it back to the van...

It was 4:15 pm when my phone rang. It was my husband, Anthony. I could barely hear him because the connection was not the best. He sounded very upset, so I told him I would call him back as soon as I had a better signal. I returned his phone call within a few minutes as we were leaving The Bluff. He reported that my mother-in-law Frances had fallen, and that the landlord had called to let him know. She had been lying there for quite some time. I told him to take a deep breath, call for an ambulance, and go to her home with Michael because I would not be home for a while. Approximately eighteen months ago, we had purchased a Life Alert for her to wear around her neck, but she had stopped wearing it. Intuitively and psychically, I had envisioned her taking a fall like this for quite some time, but having people believe in what you see and feel could happen is often not readily accepted and understood.

Our son Anthony's birthday was October 16th, and he had called to say that he was worried because his Grandma Frances had not called him for his birthday - and that he could not reach her by phone. My husband had thought nothing of it because sometimes we did not hear from her for a few days. However, our son Anthony intuitively knew that something was wrong.

My husband and Michael went to her apartment to find her lying on the floor in her feces. Unfortunately, she had fallen backwards and broken her hip. My husband and son picked her up off the floor and placed her in a chair. She wasn't making sense and speaking in fragments. They waited for an ambulance, which took some time due to Covid. While waiting, Michael called me to say how upsetting it was to find her on the floor like that. I had to calm him down by reassuring him that sometimes things just happen, and there isn't anything we could have done, except try our best, which he was doing already, and that I was proud of him.

She was taken to a local hospital. A week later, a rod was implanted in her hip. Over a two-week period, we needed to have her admitted into a rehabilitation facility. Over the course of the next three months, we could not even visit her because of the pandemic. The situation was getting to her both emotionally and mentally, and I certainly could not blame her. I am sure this also affected all of the other patients and their families. No hope of visitation is exceedingly depressing. Regrettably, she needed long-term care, which meant we needed to discuss where her needs would best be taken care of on a permanent basis. Her sister Josie was in a nursing home, and my husband's cousin Maria was a security guard there so that seemed like the best placement for her.

In the three months following her fall, we had packed up her apartment, cashed in her insurance policies, made her burial and trust arrangements, set-up a Health Care Proxy and Power of Attorney, moved her to the nursing home, and filled out her Medicaid documents. Unfortunately, her generation never really thought about preemptively handling these important issues…I found myself taking all of it on - all at once. This was a learning curve for my husband and me.

Every night, I said my prayers to be guided for the highest good for all involved and led towards the right direction and people in order to make the right decisions for her. This was just one of the difficult decisions we had to make and carry out. Sometimes you just have to keep on moving forward, reminding yourself that you are doing your best. Have faith - and eventually all will fall into place.

Chapter 16
"The Northport Residential Move"
Anthony's Forever Home?

January 4, 2021: We had been preparing for this big day for a very long time. Anthony was finally going to be moving into his forever home in Northport. Many Zoom calls and team meetings had been preparing us for this moment. Never could I have imagined that it would turn out the way it did.

We had visited the house previously on a few occasions to meet with all of the other parents and staff. All of the necessary paperwork had been filled out and was in order: social security card, insurance card, guardianship papers, open door papers, etc. We were also given a list of all of the individuals moving into the home. My son Anthony immediately mentioned to my husband, new/old staff, the Managing Director and me that he did not want his room to be next to this one particular individual. He explained that since he knew him to be a biter, he did not want his bedroom to be too close by. Anthony had a really bad feeling about it. We were all assured that this would not be a problem. We trusted them at their word, but something just did not feel right.

The new home's construction and the delivery of Anthony's bedroom set were delayed due to Covid, causing the move-in date to keep changing. Of course, all of this created so much anxiety in our home. We were trapped inside this gray area of the Unknown, which is never a good place to be…especially when you are on the spectrum.

We had made arrangements with our neighbor Matt to join us with his pick-up truck so that we could make one trip. He is a police officer with the town of Hempstead. Anthony excitedly got in the truck with him, and we were on our way. We took Montauk Highway, and the ride seemed to take forever. I had not slept well the night before. We had packed and organized all of his belongings, but for some reason, the anticipation was making me uneasy. Perhaps it was because the agency kept insisting that he move in before the holidays, (December 22nd) and this just didn't make sense to me. We waited this long already, so why not wait until after the holidays? We told them that the move would take place on January 4th.

We pulled up in front of the house and met with the Director of Adult Residential Services and the House Manager. We all grabbed containers and proceeded to enter the Northport house. Anthony, my husband, our son Michael, Matt and I walked past the kitchen, into the living room, and then towards Anthony's bedroom. Instead of being warmly greeted by the Northport staff, Anthony and three staff members were immediately bitten, attacked and lunged at by the young man about whom Anthony had expressed concerns. We saw that he could not be easily managed, was extremely aggressive, and completely out of control. Anthony had a bite mark on his shoulder that had broken his skin. I immediately brought him to the nurse's station where she put ointment and a bandage on it.

We were told that this happened because it was a new transition, and that there was too much traffic going in and out of the house. Anthony was clearly traumatized by the occurrence, and my parental instincts were giving me second thoughts concerning his safety in that house. Anthony's prior observations of this young man were indeed accurate. He had made everyone aware that this individual had very violent tendencies. Then, to make matters worse, Anthony was distraught to see that his room was in close proximity to the very individual he had asked not to be near – despite the previous promise. Due to the pandemic, most jobs, job training, day habs and all outside activities had been put on hold. This rule meant that residents would be confined to their houses for an indefinite amount of time, which would be an ongoing safety issue for everyone living there. Honestly, you really couldn't blame us, or our son, for feeling a rising sense of panic.

I did not think the day could go further downhill until we finally made it to his room after all the chaos and discovered that his bedroom furniture had not arrived. This was what I call "a clusterF@!!# of epic proportions," which is my exasperated term for an utterly disordered and mismanaged situation. (It sounds pretty accurate to me.) Since Anthony is on the autism spectrum, I wasn't quite sure how these "experts" did not realize that having him moving in without his furniture in the room would definitely be a problem. As a result, we were unable to organize his belongings, fix his bedding, etc. to give him a more comfortable feeling. So yes, the non-delivery certainly would have given us more of an impetus to move him in on a later date since we knew how it would negatively affect his emotional and mental state of being. Now, not only was he perseverating about being bitten, but he continued to be disturbed by the fact that his room was not in the order that he had expected. Anthony did not like the Residential Supervisor, and his reasons quickly became quite obvious. These children on the spectrum have a great sense of reading people's energy. She was very cold, exuding no warmth – not even a smile. Anthony confided that he felt she didn't like her job position.

We fixed his bedding and organized his room the best that we could. We reluctantly left Anthony at his new house. Before we left his room, I placed rosary beads from the Vatican that had been blessed by the Pope on his windowsill and said a few prayers for him to be safe and content in his new home. I left there with a crashing headache as well as a sinking feeling in the pit of my stomach. I cried all the way home…emotional, anxious, and without any sense of direction. Was it the right decision to leave him there?

Anthony called me every night from his cell phone to report that he was unable to sleep because of the noises coming from the room next door. He was starkly afraid of being bitten again.

The Director tried to reassure us that everyone on the team was committed to providing a safe and happy environment for Anthony as well as for all of his housemates in the Northport house. She kept reiterating that it was unfortunate Anthony's move-in day was not as smooth as we all would have liked. She told us that she had met with the team the following morning to establish better routines and structure, which would improve the situation considerably. She continued her list of positives by mentioning staff retraining sessions pertaining to behavior interventions for the other individual. In addition, she wanted us to know that the Supervisor of Crisis Intervention was spending a lot of time at the house to train the staff on how to implement the behavior plans and provide redirection. There were also a considerable number of therapists involved in providing the role-modeling, supervision, observation, feedback, and training needed to ensure the success of Anthony and the other residents who were now experiencing a new sense of independence in their adult lives. However, Anthony never felt reassured at all - even with all the new programs being implemented. He firmly believed that if the staff had had difficulties controlling this young man's behavior before the move, it surely wasn't going to happen now. Unfortunately, Anthony's intuition was correct; the situation escalated to a frightening level.

On my birthday, January 7th, I awoke with an unsettling feeling that I needed to take my son away from that house. It was not that I could pinpoint a reason. Call it a mother's intuition. The first call was to my friend Sharon who, without hesitation, told me to go get him. She always trusts my instincts. Both of us shared stories of the Virgin Mary and our strong faith in her. Why would she question me now? My husband, who could read my face instinctively, said, "Let's get ready and go get him." On the drive there, I spoke with my friend Linda, another special needs mom. She asked if I had received and read the most recent email from the agency explaining that all residences were going to be on lockdown due to the Coronavirus. I told her I had not, but that was all the more reason for us to bring him home with us. He was continuing to experience severe anxiety because he did not feel that he, or anyone else living there was protected from danger. He was also concerned about the troubled young man because he had always considered him to be a friend. Anthony knew this boy needed a lot more support than he was getting.

We arrived at the house, collected Anthony, his meds, Xbox and clothing. We told the staff that we would let them know when he would be returning. On the drive home, he described a horrific incident that had occurred. That same troubled young man had sat down on the floor and began consuming raw pork as the staff observed without doing anything to stop him. Anthony was under the impression that the staff was afraid of him because of his aggressive behavior. He clearly had these same issues at the previous residence, and it was continuing at the Northport home. After listening to our son and the troublesome situation that had occurred, (and due to the pandemic restrictions as I had mentioned before), we decided to keep Anthony at home with us.

The next day, I sent an email to the entire team explaining that our concerns had escalated. Since my son no longer felt safe in what was supposed to be his permanent home, we would be keeping him home with us indefinitely until another placement became available. According to the agency, this individual could not be removed or named according to HIPPA regulations. As Anthony's mother, I thought this was totally ridiculous! Anthony was so concerned, not only for his own well-being and safety, but also for his friends that he had grown up with and now lived in the home. He also continued to be worried for the young man who had bitten him, but who desperately needed help. Even with everything that took place, Anthony still considered him a friend. What a compassionate son we have raised! Obviously, my son was not the problem, but because Anthony no longer felt safe in the home - and the young man's behaviors could not be controlled, there was no choice but for Anthony to leave.

As a parent, this situation took its toll on my conscience. I needed to report it to the New York State Justice Center. The Justice Center is committed to supporting and protecting the health, safety, and dignity of all people with special needs and disabilities through advocacy of their civil rights, prevention of mistreatment, and investigation of all allegations of abuse and neglect so that appropriate actions are taken.[i] After registering our complaint, my son was able to communicate what had taken place to them all on his own. We also received a phone call from the compliance department of the agency affiliated with the home and OPWDD (Office for People with Developmental Disabilities), which is responsible for coordinating services for New Yorkers with developmental disabilities. OPWDD called to see if they could help implement services for Anthony while he was with us, but since there were no services at the time because of the virus, there was nothing that could be done except wait until another home placement was available.

After this heart wrenching and troubling experience, I realized that the adult group home system was broken – and truly frightening. I was thinking about all the stories that had been confided to me by other parents, and now I was living the same nightmare. Ugh! I knew I had given this crisis my all, and now I needed to learn how to let go.

I had weekly Zoom calls with the Managing Director and leadership team, which were ongoing for a few months. Most of the homes and their suggestions did not come to fruition, either due to Covid delays or no availability.

During the first week of April 2021, we received a phone call from the Managing Director from another agency because we had decided to actively look and expand the search outside our previous agency. There was an opening in the Moriches, located on the east end of Long Island. We were sent photos of the home by email, and it seemed perfect. Now we needed to set up an intake interview via Zoom to see if Anthony would be a suitable match. I knew that he would be…and he was. The intake interview went off without a hitch. As I watched Anthony conduct himself, I was very impressed. It was not at all surprising that they loved him. He was an ideal match. The residents consisted of five young men and six young ladies. We were all thrilled about his new beginning and began coordinating a visit with the staff and agency.

On April 14th, we took Anthony for his tour of the Moriches home, and it was just as beautiful and immaculate as its pictures. We were welcomed by Melissa and Tracy, the house managers. The entire staff was incredibly warm and welcoming. We were introduced to all of the housemates, who were also openly friendly. The home was divided in half, with one side holding the ladies' bedrooms, and the other consisting of the men's bedrooms. There was a huge kitchen with bright sunlight shining through the back glass doors, a large living room with seating area, an expansive recreation area in the basement, and a built-in swimming pool with a shaded barbeque area, which was soon to be renovated for use the following summer. I could see and feel my son Anthony's happiness. After all we had been through, this was well worth the wait. Now we just needed to coordinate a move-in date, which we soon learned would be May 3, 2021.

At the end of this chapter, I realize that while one door had closed, something entirely better was waiting for us. God had another wonderful plan and a new beginning for Anthony. Although we couldn't see it, and it wasn't tangible, it existed. You must have faith, patience, and hope for all things to fall into place. As soon as I relinquished needing to control the situation, the doors opened freely. This is called divine timing, which is the belief that everything in your life happens at exactly the right moment. Although life's events may seem overwhelming, unusual, or even nonsensical, divine timing assures you that the Universe is placing people, objects, challenges and more into your life when you can handle them.

With a very heavy heart, I must disclose that the troubled young man who had resided at Anthony's Northport home passed away from pneumonia a short time after Anthony moved into his new home in the Moriches. May God's peace shine upon him…

[i] **www.justicecenter.ny.gov**

Chapter 17
"Dad Goes to the Hospital"
The Beginning of the End

April 20, 2021: Started off much like any other day, but this day would turn out to be like no other. Every morning, I have a cup of coffee and make two very important phone calls — the first to my mom and the second to my BFF Patty. My mom was in her early stages of dementia, and Patty had been diagnosed with kidney disease. This morning, my mom shares that for the past few evenings while my dad was trying to sleep, his breathing was very labored. Two years earlier, during a spiritual session with Terry Lauria, I had been foretold about my dad's heart condition, and my parents' future financial issues, which confirmed my own forebodings at that time.

At the same time, I had also been discussing with Patty my fears of dad having heart issues, while also feeling empathy for him and his heart. I knew intuitively that the Universe was preparing me with the strength I would need for the inevitable. In addition, I had known for a while that my parents were definitely not prepared for what was coming and were in financial difficulties because of their lack of planning. During my call with Patty, she told me to remain calm, meditate, be patient and see how the day went. My dad was a loving man, always smiling, but not an easy man when it concerned his health. On April 8th, his medical doctor had ordered some testing done and then to follow up with a cardiologist.

At eighty-four years of age, my dad was set in his ways, remaining a heavy smoker with a strong aversion to any medical testing and/or medications. He had no faith in chemical interventions, but did believe in eating organically, which meant soaking his meats, vegetables, and fruits in apple cider vinegar and baking soda. He also drank a concoction of kale, pineapple, ginger, spinach, honey, and turmeric every morning, afternoon, and evening.

I remember that day as having been extremely busy for me. My son Anthony was moving into his forever home on May 3rd, and so I was getting his belongings and paperwork together. In the afternoon I had a hair appointment, but all day I just could not help but feel a huge knot in the pit of my stomach that just wouldn't unravel. Even getting my hair done did not make me feel better. It was almost as if I knew what was coming - I had been feeling uneasy about my dad throughout the prior months leading up to this day. As I sat in the salon chair, Spirit also let me know that my sons needed to spend more quality time with him in the upcoming months.

That evening, while cleansing my face, I felt an urgency to call my parents. I could hear the panic in my mom's voice as she described my dad struggling to breathe. I told her to hand him the phone… I could barely make out his words. I managed to make him understand that we would be taking him to the nearest hospital. I woke up my husband, and we ran out of the house in our flannels, driving straight to my parents' home. As we pulled up to the house, my dad was waiting in the front hallway. His face was pale, his skin was clammy, and he was definitely presenting with hyperpnea. I was very scared, so I began to say the Lord's Prayer under my breath. He did not want an ambulance. That's all he kept repeating. My husband drove. I sat with him in the back seat of the car, held his hand, told him to breathe in through his nose and out through his mouth. We passed St. Joseph's, the local hospital on Hempstead Turnpike - so yes, I lied to him. I whispered to my husband that he should drive directly to St. Francis Hospital, which is recognized for its excellence in cardiac health. My husband, being an experienced driver, put the pedal to the metal and we made it there in no time.

My husband dropped my dad and me at the emergency room entrance. I walked in slowly with my dad's hand in mine. The emergency room staff was shocked at my dad's strength: he was gasping for breath yet remained strong - walking steadily on his feet. In the midst of filling out his paperwork, I needed to take my beta-blocker and Xanax for my own heart issues and anxieties. I helped my dad remove his coat, and suddenly realized how old and frail he had become. So true what they say - our roles were now reversed. The nurse placed the hospital bracelet on him. I told my dad I would stay as long as they would let me, but he would need major testing to be conducted there. The radiologist came to escort him from the emergency room front office. My dad proceeded to walk with him because he did not want to be taken away in a wheelchair. As they both walked down what seemed like a very long hallway, my dad turned around to look for me. My heart sank. I became so emotional. Was he going to be ok? Would I ever see him again? My dad, my everything. Under my breath, I pleaded with God to let him survive this. The nurse told us we should leave because there was not much we could do at this point, and the Covid restrictions were still very much in place. We called my mom and siblings from the car and decided to leave because there was not much else we could do.

My dad remained in the hospital for ten days. During his stay, he was diagnosed with atrial fibrillation, congestive heart failure, COPD, pulmonary disease, and kidney issues. He also needed to have a catheter because he could not urinate on his own and was retaining fluids due to his heart and kidney issues. He was prescribed seven medications and an inhaler. I was both my parents' healthcare proxies. I was hypersensitive and anxious in making these critical decisions for them, even though I have had to retain medical information regarding medications and procedures for my son Anthony. As such, I am used to running on adrenaline and having "fight-or-flight syndrome." The only difference now was that this was life or death.

I also had to relay this information to my siblings in what I called the "dreaded family group text message," and found myself being questioned constantly by them about my communications with the health professionals, which only increased my anxiety. My brothers and I did not communicate very often, but that was not due to our lack of trying. We socialized mostly at the elaborate holiday parties given at my brother's home with his friends. Now we spoke on a daily basis, which heightened everyone's emotions and lack of self-control. One of my brothers just needed to have control over everything. He kept berating me about all my decisions, causing my stress levels to become even more unsurmountable. I had to agree that being the healthcare proxy for both my parents, as well acting as their power of attorney, was simply too overwhelming a responsibility. As such, I decided to pass our parents' financial responsibilities on to my brother. This way, I could focus on their medical needs and what required my immediate attention. My brother was an entrepreneur, so that only rendered my decision more sensible. More importantly, let's not forget the attention I owed to my own family - and in particular, my sons' disabilities and all that those entailed.

My dad was scheduled to come home on April 30th. In the interim, as per my conversation with the social worker, we needed to find 24-hour care for both my parents, along with making sure their home was handicap-accessible. All these life changes created severe stress, which then escalated my mom's dementia level. Suddenly, my brothers and I were in charge of all their care and basic daily needs. It became very evident that one person could not handle everything. My brother found a home healthcare company called "Friends for Life," which became a huge blessing for us. We were introduced to our parents' home health care aid, Pauline, who was a Godsend. Of course, my parents were stubbornly reluctant about accepting any help from a stranger. They were convinced they could manage on their own by taking care of one another.as they always had. As they got to know Pauline however, she easily became part of our family.

Unfortunately, with my dad being home again, everything was becoming more emotional and challenging by the day. He was not cooperative about taking his meds, going to doctor appointments, etc. I would pick up my dad's medications from the pharmacy and have to hide in their basement to sort his meds. If I was discovered, he would curse and tell me he was not going to put that poison in his body. Then my mom would have hurtful outbursts with me every time I visited. It was all too mentally and emotionally exhausting. My beautiful loving mom, with whom I had had a warm and loving relationship, now seemed to hate me for making these difficult decisions to benefit them. She would scream profanities, accuse me of being a thief, call me a liar, and tell me she did not like me anymore. She had difficulty accepting the fact that my brother was taking care of their finances because they were no longer capable. Pauline would reassure me by explaining it was the illness yelling at me, and not my mother. She advised me to have her seen by a doctor who would put her on medications to calm her down. Pauline is compassionate, strong, patient, empathetic, loving, kind, insightful, and has a great sense of humor. It takes a very special person to do what she does on a daily basis.

Having my dad home was stressful on all of us. He confused his days and nights. I had to coordinate all the physical therapy, social worker, and nursing appointments for at home visits. My dad wanted to be that strong, independent, resilient man he used to be in his mind, but his body would not let him. I had my cell phone on all the time, day and night, on my nightstand near my bed. On a few occasions he had attempted walking to the bathroom at night on his own, when his blood pressure would drop so low that he would fall on the floor. Pauline would keep her ears open so she could shadow or assist him, but his ego would not allow it. Since he was on blood thinners, I would then have to get him to the hospital to make sure there was no internal bleeding or anemia. He also suffered from severe abdominal pain, catheter issues and UTI infections. I was helplessly watching my dad deteriorate in front of my eyes. The first man I ever loved, who had always protected me, now needed me to take care of him. My days and nights became a blend of my sitting in the emergency room, watching the medical professionals look for veins to put in a line for intravenous antibiotics, multiple blood transfusions, changing his catheter, collecting urine and blood samples, and testing for Covid. All I could do was repeat the Lord's Prayer and ask my angels to both intervene on his behalf and guide those medical professionals.

It just seemed impossible trying to maintain his health at home while he was in and out of hospitals every few months. I found myself doubting my decision-making constantly, even though I knew I was being divinely and intuitively guided. After discussing it with both my brothers, we decided there really was no choice: he needed to be placed in a nursing home rehab facility. We all felt as if we had been punched in the face. I handled all the preliminary paperwork - and we would wait and see what progress he would make in ninety days. We settled upon a facility – and held our breath.

For the first two months, my dad made progress, but Covid restrictions threw us a wicked curveball. We were now allowed to visit only once a week and limited to two visitors for a half hour. In July, one of the patients tested positive with Covid and it all went downhill from there. I would set up Zoom meetings for my parents, but the videos only made his decline even more obvious. Sadly, he was of sound mind, and so it became increasingly difficult for him to remain there. I felt in my heart that he was giving up on himself. He would call me a few times a week and ask when he could come home. This went on for quite a few weeks- it was emotionally destroying me inside. My only solace was that we had renovated our backyard into a beautiful outside living space and sanctuary. It had a full kitchen, fire pits, swimming pool, and sitting and eating area. It could not have come at a better time. The Universe knew what it was that I needed to feed and fuel my soul, along with the love and support of family and my soul tribe. There is always something to be grateful for if you look for it. There is always a silver lining.

In early September, I received a phone call from the nursing home wanting to discuss the dreadful DNR, (Do Not Resuscitate), which means that if his heart gave out, the medical team would allow the natural process of death to occur. It was one of the most difficult things to comprehend. My brothers and I had to coordinate compassion visits. My dad would call for my mom every two minutes to make sure she was at his side. Being married for fifty-nine years, all they had ever known was each other's company.

During one of those Compassion or End-of-Life visits, a nurse or aide mentioned to my brother that since they were short staffed, maybe it was time for my dad to come home. Not once did I ever feel my dad was abused or neglected. My dad wanted to come home to die, but I was hesitant. I feared that his returning home would exacerbate my mother's dementia and health even further. I was extremely afraid of losing both my parents. I was told that I was selfish, but that accusation could not have been any further from the truth. It was decided that my dad was to come home on September 9th with hospice care. My brother fought with me to be our dad's healthcare proxy, but I felt he was just too emotional and illogical for that role. I had learned the value of separating emotions from logic by raising two disabled sons.

I had an epiphany one afternoon while speaking to my mentor and spiritual advisor, Terry Lauria. When my dad came home, I could bring my mom out with me to relieve some of her stress caused by his condition. However, a family member needed to be present to give pain medications. So instead, I would visit my mom, speak with Pauline, and sit with my dad to make sure his needs were being met.

One afternoon while visiting, the social worker arrived at the same time. She assessed how my dad was doing, approached me, and asked what my thoughts were. I told her that he calls for my mom every three to five minutes. I believed that he was passing to the other side and coming back into his earthly body because he needed to know that she was here for him. My mother would get up constantly, falling a few times because she thought it was her responsibility to make him better by taking care of him and all his needs as she had always done. This went on even though she could not even manage to take care of herself, which left her very vulnerable and a major safety concern. The social worker gently explained that it was important for us to tell him it was ok to leave us. I understood that this final goodbye was going to be mine. I had sat with my dad so many times exchanging what was in my heart... I knew what it was I needed to do.

Upon awakening on September 18th, I felt compelled to visit my parents and take my mom out with my cousin Donna. This did not feel like any ordinary day. When arriving at their home, I asked my mom if she wanted to go with my dad or stay here with us. It was something that just came out of my mouth. She said she wanted to stay here. I looked at her, took a deep breath, and said, "Well then, Donna is coming over and we are taking you out for the day. Reservations have been made at the Milleridge Inn, and we are going to spend the afternoon together." While Pauline got her ready and we were waiting for Donna, I decided to sit with my dad for a little while to speak with him in private. I held his hand and thanked him for being a good man, dad, and grandfather. I reassured him that both his grandsons were doing well, and that he had done a great job. I told him that I would try and get along with both my brothers - even though I knew in my heart that would be a major challenge. Lastly, Mom would be taken care of by all of us.

"Dad, it's ok for you to leave. I know that you are tired. You will always be the first man I ever loved. Now Donna and I are taking mom out for a few hours." We spent four hours having lunch together, talking, laughing, walking, and taking pictures. My mom was taking in the air and enjoying the sun on her face, as she smiled with a deep appreciation for being given the emotional and mental break that she needed so badly. The Milleridge Inn was decorated for Halloween. You could smell fresh pumpkin and cinnamon in the air as we walked towards the bakery. We picked up a fresh cinnamon bread roll for my mom to bring home. She then simply said, "Thank you for my day… it's time to go back home."

I dreaded taking her home. My mom was happy, so I tried not to show my emotions because I knew the inevitable was unfolding. As I walked my mom into her house, I removed her jacket and sat her in an armchair in the living room. I walked back into the bedroom, kissed my dad between the eyes, and told him that I loved him. The room started to get brighter. I saw a bright light above his body. I went and opened the bedroom window so his spirit could be free. Leaving him… and with no regrets, I knew that evening would be my last one spent with my beloved father.

Chapter 18
"The Moriches Move"
YAY! Anthony's Forever Home

May 3, 2021: Woohoo today's the day! My heart is practically jumping out of my chest. Our baby is moving into his forever home. There are so many emotions attached to this moment, but I will try my best to put them into words. As a parent, I'm so excited for him…even more thrilling is the knowledge that he is ready. That oh-so-young complex 7-year-old child who moved out of our home years ago is now a mature independent 22-year-old man-child, eager to start a new journey into the next level of his life. Our Northport experience wasn't the best, but intuitively I knew this move would be the right one for all of us.

Anthony had shown some serious signs of PTSD (Post Traumatic Stress Disorder) after the biting incident in the Northport house. As a result, we had decided to pick up his belongings, and bring Anthony home until a better placement became available. This decision gave us time to reorganize his things and prepare him for his final move to the Moriches, a beautiful seascape community on eastern Long Island. We had so many delays and difficulties because of Covid restrictions, but Anthony remained calm and confident. I discussed the delays caused by the virus with him quite often, and he seemed to understand the circumstances. More importantly, he knew was not alone in this new Covid world. Everyone was going through the same ordeal – some worse than others. He realized this harsh truth and understood that he was a part of something bigger now.

The night before his move, we brought up all of his labeled containers and placed them in the dining area. Our neighbor Matt arrived at our home at 10:00 am with his truck to help move Anthony into his new home. Matt is one of my son's favorite people. My husband, Michael, Matt and I packed the truck, stopping at Dunkin' Donuts for breakfast. We headed out onto Sunrise Highway…we were embarking on a new adventure together!

My overall nervous anticipation gave me butterflies in my stomach. All of our many years of sacrifice were coming to fruition. My mind was racing with thoughts that there were still so many wonderful things that could happen for us, despite the virus. I felt exceedingly grateful for this opportunity for all of us. Here was our silver lining, which I was seeing, feeling, and experiencing completely.

We pulled up in front of his new home, and were immediately greeted by the residential managers, staff members and residents. We all grabbed containers, lined up, got our temperatures checked, and donned our masks before entering the house. Anthony led the way, following Melissa, (the Residential Manager) to his new room. This time the transition went off without any problems whatsoever. Michael hooked up Anthony's Xbox, laptop, phone, and then connected all the electronics with the Wi-Fi password. We got busy organizing his clothing in the closet and drawers, hanging up his posters, placing his new Pokémon comforter on his bed, and labeling his toiletries in the bathroom. He hugged all of us, took some pictures and told us, "You can all go now." It was such a bittersweet moment. Our son is all grown up now. Flashbacks of our leaving him so many years earlier at that first residence catapulted into my brain - Anthony dressed as Harry Potter, waving his wand. Catching my breath, I turned away as he was talking to his new adult friends and peers.

As we were leaving, my husband opened the car door and hugged me. Under his breath, he looked into my eyes and asked, "Are you ok, my love?" My response, spoken with bravado, was "Yes, this is the moment we've been waiting for - Babe, we did it!" As we were pulling away from his home, I took one more look over my shoulder, and felt a strong sense of contentment come over me. I welcomed this day as Anthony's new beginning – the first of many successful ones to come. Unlike the first, this moving day was one of quiet bliss, built upon hope.

Now we needed to address Michael's melancholy over his brother's new move. I saw Michael struggling to hold back his tears and conflicting emotions for his brother. I asked Michael if he wanted to discuss it and he said, "I'm so happy for him and for you both as my parents, but I'm also sad for myself because I'm really going to miss him. Sure, he's a pain in the ass, but he's my pain in the ass and I love him!" Then he blurted out, "Who's going to play Pokémon with me now?" During the pandemic, Anthony and Michael had become so very close; the bond between them was evident to everyone around them... one of the many blessings that unexpectedly emerged out of the pandemic.

In hindsight, the path chosen for Anthony was the best decision for us as a family unit. He had now grown into an adult who was able to function in a society where being different isn't always accepted - and extremely challenging. So today I pat myself on the back as I acknowledge that he is becoming the young man I always knew he could be. I am extremely grateful for all of his accomplishments, big and small. He is seizure- free, communicative, expressive — (using curse words appropriately and within context), with a contagious sense of humor, compassion, empathy, and a fierce love to all who are kind and respectful towards him. He has a lot more to accomplish, but it's within his reach. God has his hand in everything, and in everything - there is God. Hope and faith keep you on your mark. Don't lose sight even when all seems impossible.

Here is a reminder to those who are struggling: sometimes blocks and detours are just reroutes to something even better and that's exactly what happened to us. God and the Universe had a better plan for Anthony and our family. It was very difficult when we were in the gray area, but we trusted the process. In the end, holding onto our faith thrust us into the right steps for attaining a better outcome.

Chapter 19
"Dad Passes Away"
The Dreadful Funeral

September 19, 2021: I woke up to three missed phone calls on my cell. For some odd reason, I had shut my cell phone off that night before going to bed - not that I have any explanation for doing so. My home phone rang; it seemed louder than usual... I heard my sister-in-law Cathy's quivering voice telling me to go to my parents' home. She warned that the situation was not good. Time stood still. As I wash my face and brush my teeth, I am struck by the thought that life is indeed too short. It had only been the night before that I had prayed on my knees for the Lord to take my dad and release him from his pain. On the way to their home, I sensed that my dad was gone. What was normally a twenty-minute ride felt like forever because of all of the dizzying thoughts running through my head.

Upon arrival, I see my siblings and spouses sitting in front of the house. My sister-in-law Maria holds me close and tells me softly that my dad had passed. I walk into the house, down the narrow hallway, into their bedroom to find my mom sitting next to the bed, holding my dad's hand, with Pauline quietly observing from the other side. My dad has a light grey pale look to him, but he is no longer crying out in pain.

Then it was necessary to remove my mom away from the harsh reality of his death, to shield her from the all-encompassing trauma that Death entails: the examination of the body by the hospice staff, the death certificate, the final removal of the body from their home. I called my mom's sister, Aunt Cathy, and my cousin Donna to tell them the devastating news. Both decided to arrange to be with my mom so that my brothers and I could make funeral arrangements. From the beginning, Aunt Cathy unwaveringly supported me through this very difficult life-changing process.

Suddenly, I needed space… lots of space to think and process everything. I felt such a heaviness in my chest. I walked to the side of the house and looked through the back side gate where I saw two individuals pushing the stretcher and placing my dad's body in the back of an ordinary SUV. I couldn't feel my legs, breathlessly falling to the ground, crying uncontrollably. My husband Anthony first tried to help me get back on my feet and off the ground, but my body had crumpled into a dead weight. So, he patiently sat next to me on the ground with my head on his shoulder for a while. He kept repeating that everything was going to be ok.

After I had allowed myself the time to completely collapse in grief, I began to pull myself together for the sake of my mom. Now it came time to pick out his final wardrobe: black suit with fine white pinstripes, pink shirt with his name Armando inscribed on the inside, purple and pink paisley tie, and black shoes. My brothers brought his things to the funeral home and made the arrangements. I stayed behind to keep a watchful eye on my mom. At one point she forgot my dad had passed and went to visit him in their bedroom. That was heart-wrenching to watch.

As we sat in the yard eating bagels and drinking coffee with my mom, my cousin Donna asked her if she had a simple black dress to wear for the funeral. I'm wondering how life will continue without our paternal mainstay? I feel a coldness inside. Donna and I went shopping…the world did not stop spinning or pause because my dad was no longer with us. The silence of his not being there was deafening - and this would be just the beginning.

After we were done shopping, we met back at the house with my brothers who had made the funeral arrangements. We had already depleted my parents' savings very quickly due to my dad's medical and home healthcare costs. My mom had cashed in their life insurance policies in advance and put my name on their bank accounts months before he got ill so that she and I could pay and pre-plan their future funeral arrangements. Unfortunately, that day never took place because we had had to use those funds for other necessary bills. However, we were fortunate enough to have my brother cover the funeral expenses.

Together as a family, we began discussing readings at the mass, pallbearers, limousines, what was to be displayed, etc. My nieces were speaking about what they would place in the coffin with him: a deck of cards because he loved poker, a pack of cigarettes, and rosary beads. I was too tired and emotionally drained to really concentrate, but I felt there was something he would want to take with him that we had forgotten.

On the morning of the funeral, I sat on my bed and started a conversation with my dad as I stared at his picture. I closed my eyes and asked him if there was anything he would like to take with him that we had missed. I saw him clearly showing me his Italian First Communion Bible that was held together with tape. I called Aunt Cathy, who was there to help my mom get dressed and for whatever else was needed. I asked her to please look in the nightstand for his Bible that had the memorial cards from his siblings and family tucked inside of it. "Please bring it to the funeral home because he wants to take it with him." She never questioned my reasoning. This was his sacred bible, which he read and prayed with every evening before bed.

We spoke with the funeral director and had her place the bible and other sentimental objects in his coffin. I find it to be so strange that the person is no longer physically here except in spirit, and yet all of his belongings and material things remain here. While we work so hard for those things in life, in the end all we keep are the memories and the love we have in our hearts.

My dad was loved and respected by so many that it was standing room only throughout the entire funeral. The room was filled with such beautiful flower arrangements, memorial gifts, mass cards, etc. My cousin, Monsignor Edward, traveled from New Jersey to say a few words in memory of him. Certain personal memories stood out: his excellent work as a steamfitter and plumber, his big bright smile, his hard-working hands always holding a cigarette, his dedication to those in need, his cooking skills, his avoidance of arguments or confrontation, and loving peace instead. If he didn't like you, you knew it! My mom was the love of his life, and his family, children and grandchildren were always his top priority. I've never heard anyone say an unkind word about him. When he was provoked, he spoke out, but he never spoke unpleasantly about anyone that wasn't the truth. Come to think of it, the apple did not fall too far from the tree…

September 23rd was a Thursday - the day my dad was laid to rest. We all arrived at the funeral home a half an hour early to say our farewells and to close the coffin. I stood on one side of my mother, with my brothers on the other, walking and supporting her. We were in that room (that felt so claustrophobic) surrounding my dad to give him our last respects. It was an extraordinarily tense time for everyone. My heart was thumping when my brother unexpectedly insisted on keeping my dad's bible. I couldn't understand his reason. This bible did not belong to him. He was given my dad's wedding band…why now the bible too? I told him, "No it doesn't belong to you - it belongs with dad. It is his and he wants to take it with him."

In the midst of all this chaotic conflict, it is time for my sons to say goodbye to their grandfather. I watch on the sidelines as I see Michael look searchingly into his brother's eyes, before quietly explaining: "Do you understand what it means to say your final goodbye to Grandpa? He isn't coming back. There is no respawn like in video games, Anthony. You get it, right?" Anthony looks directly back at Michael and solemnly responds, "Yes, there is no respawn." (When a character in an online game is given another life after dying.)[i] Their interaction gave me chills.

After the funeral director had a conversation with my mom and Aunt Cathy, the bible remained with my dad and the subject, and the coffin were closed. Clearly, my brother was very annoyed with the decision that was made. I fumed because I felt that not only was I experiencing this enormous loss, but now I was being forced to contend with negative behaviors on so many levels... I'm wondering if there is a lesson to be learned here.

Emotions are now running high, and I'm struggling to hold back my tears because I know I will need a great deal of strength on this day of all days. We gathered outside to meet by the limousines to take us to the mass. In our limousine was Aunt Cathy, Anthony, my sons Anthony and Michael, my mother, and her aide Pauline. I was relieved to remember that small but crucial interaction between my sons. Throughout this very trying experience, Michael and Anthony had been emotionally stable, carrying themselves like mature young men. I felt so much sadness for the loss of my dad, but so very proud of the way my sons handled themselves. They remained together and supported one another through it all. What more could a parent ask for?

Parts of the funeral mass remain a blur to me, very much like an out of body experience. I didn't really feel grounded. I walked in, supporting my mom with my sisters-in-law to the front pew. My sons, husband and brothers carried the casket into the church. All I really remember was the priest talking about my dad, his home in the province of Frosinone, Italy - and the social gatherings we all enjoyed. My dad would always lift his glass on these occasions and proclaim his favorite toast, "To those that wish us well, the rest can go to hell!" Fine wine, mediocre wine, cheap wine, any wine, it never mattered. As long as we were together enjoying the good food and each other, it was always a special occasion.

My dad was raised by a single mom. Her name was Margherita. His dad passed away when he was two years old from a massive heart attack. My grandmother raised him and his four siblings on her own - two sisters and two brothers. She was a woman of faith with a soul of fire who traveled to America by ship, on the Andrea Doria - without a husband - to give her family a better life. Talk about strength! Her faith in God was fierce. She said God was all the man she needed in her life. My dad was the last of his nuclear family to cross over the ocean. I envisioned my grandmother making homemade pasta, the brothers playing cards, drinking wine and smoking, and his sisters baking. That was the image I held in my mind's eye as I left the church…and I was good with that.

I was very concerned for my mother's mental and emotional health during that day, but she was holding her own. As we were leaving the church, I felt relieved that my dad wasn't suffering any more. No one wants to see their loved one in excruciating pain.

My dad was laid to rest in a mausoleum in Pinelawn Cemetery, the day before his 85th birthday, surrounded by all of his family members. The love there was so overwhelming. What a beautiful resting place. It was filled with such deep earth colors. A huge pine tree sat in the center of the mausoleum which grew all the way through to the top of the glass opening. I had never seen anything so breathtaking. He was at peace and there was no more agony.

We ended the day with a huge Italian meal with the entire family, much as we had enjoyed so many times in the past, but what I really wanted to do was crawl in a ball and go to bed. It was all too exhausting, and I just wanted it all to end. I always say I want to be celebrated when I pass, and now I understand why my wishes may be difficult for some to fulfill. My dad would not want anyone crying and mourning over him. He would say he had a good long life and was now ready to move on. "Wake up and live!' he would say.

Grief comes in waves. Some days are better than others. It could be a song, a meal, or a visit from an animal that reminds you of that person. Anytime, anywhere you could be in a pool of tears with absolutely no warning. I once read that grief is like living two lives. One is where you pretend that everything is alright. The other is where your heart screams silently in pain. That sounds about accurate.

One of the biggest misconceptions is, "Blood makes you family." No, blood makes you related; loyalty, love, respect and trust make you family. You are not obligated to have relationships with family members who are not beneficial for your mental health. Respect is for those who deserve it, not for those who demand it. I also realized the one thing I absolutely love and adore about myself is that no matter how badly I've been treated, no matter how I'm feeling, no matter what I've been through or what I'm going through, I still have a heart of gold and endless love and light to give others. That's the one thing no one can ever take from me. The harsh truth is that being good to others doesn't guarantee that others will be good to you, but that will never change who I am and worked so very hard to become. My dad would always remind me of how wise and strong I was. I will always take that belief with me…especially on my darkest days.

[i] Collins English Dictionary, Harper Collins Publishers

Chapter 20
"Mom has Dementia"
I Just Remembered I Love You

October 2021: Unfortunately, as my dad's illness began to take hold of him, my mother's dementia escalated. She had fallen and hit her head in a previous year, which may have acted as a catalyst. When someone you love has dementia, you will both go through intense feelings of grief and loss, which are some of the most difficult emotions with which to contend. When you are close to a person with dementia, you will be struck by waves of deep loss and sorrow without warning - usually around the time of their diagnosis, as the disease progresses, and eventually towards the end of their life. Death itself, or even the fear of death, does not bring on this sense of bereavement. Death is always there, standing between you, never allowing you to forget. It is known as "The Long Goodbye."[i]

I'm certain my mom shares my feelings of loss and grief over her condition because she is no longer able to find the words to express herself. My mom has always been a strong, intelligent, caring, and outspoken woman. Being of European descent though, she was also dependent upon my dad and he was no longer here. They spent over fifty-four years together. Physical skills that had come easily to her before were now becoming exceedingly more difficult to accomplish. Moreover, her fear of falling has become uppermost in her mind, pushing out everything else.

Dementia is progressive and life-shortening. There are so many changes hitting her from all sides…all at once. It must be like trying to make your way through a carnival fun house, except for the fact that you do not find it funny. At times, my mom can become seriously angry and irrational. She cannot cope with the reality that she is no longer in control. She screams profanities at me, tells me I'm trying to take over her life, and that I am stealing from her. She still maintains she could live in the house alone without any assistance, despite the hard evidence.

Grief is the natural reaction to loss. Sadness and distress intensify, especially when the loss is significant, like the loss of a spouse. It's a very personal process. We all grieve in different ways, which include shock, despair, social withdrawal, anger, frustration, guilt, denial, desire for them, and depression. I have to admit that I have felt every one of these emotions – along with relief that my dad wasn't suffering any longer. Now I'm grieving for my mom, who is alive, but still longing for the person she was. When you love someone with dementia, you grieve for that person, your relationship with the person, companionship, support and understanding, communication you've had in the past, activities done together, and remorse over what the future could have been.

I have always spent quality time with my parents, and they have always been involved in mine and my children's lives. As such, I mourn the physical and emotional loss of my dad. Now that I am spending quality time alone with mom, I have been forced to begin the mourning process for her much too soon.

One day in October 2021, a few weeks after my father passed, I was asked to go food shopping for my mom. Since we spent so much time together, I knew what she enjoyed eating. Due to her upbringing in post-war Europe, she didn't always have enough food to eat and had painful memories of being hungry as a child. Not having food in the fridge would now exacerbate her feelings of having no control, making her even more anxious. In the past, she would spend hours cooking in the kitchen. It was my parents' passion - their way of expressing their love to all who gathered in their home. They would cook for family gatherings and holidays for up to thirty or forty people. I was thinking of all this as I was food shopping…how my mom worked a full-time job, came home exhausted, and still cooked a warm meal for us, no questions asked. Sometimes this regimen frustrated me because I wanted to spend time with her when she came home, and I felt that she wasn't emotionally available for me. Now that I have children of my own, I understand. All of these ideas and memories bubbled up in my brain from this one trip to the grocery store.

Shopping for groceries took me approximately two hours. It was emotionally exhausting and cathartic. I was afraid of disappointing her if I didn't buy exactly what she liked, or if I had forgotten something. I'm sure it also stemmed from my childhood goal of never wanting to disappoint her.

When I finally bagged and finished paying for the groceries, I could feel my eyes starting to well up with tears. Was this my new reality? My parents did everything together, and now I'm shopping for her. She's probably waiting for me to arrive by the front door. I'm concerned because she's unstable on her feet. She could be very stubborn when she wants to do something…even when it's not in her best interest.

I put the groceries in my car, put my seatbelt on, and heard a song from The Monkees called "Tear Drop City." My dad's nickname for me was "Monkey." I experienced goosebumps on the back of my neck. I knew he was with me in the car, knowing how sad I felt. Weirdly, it was a comforting thought. I allowed one brief tear to flow down my face, took a deep breath, and drove to my parents' home.

As I pulled into the driveway, there she was - standing in the hallway by the door, just as I had pictured her in my mind. I got out of the car, opened the trunk and waved hello. I saw the aide standing behind her, probably because of her instability on her feet and her forgetfulness to use her cane. I brought all the groceries in the house and helped unpack them.

As I finished, my mom looked at me and said, "I just remembered that I love you." She gave me a tight hug and big kiss. This would become a core memory for me…a deeply poignant memory that would remain significant to us both. I knew I would remember that moment all the while her dementia progressed and would eventually take her life.

As I drove away, I would think of the many previous times I would visit. Both my parents would stand by the door, together, side-by-side, and wave good-bye. As I looked in my rearview mirror, I saw my mom standing alone, waving and blowing me kisses.

[i] <u>Alzheimer's Disease and 'The Long Goodbye' | Alzheimer's Disease Research Center (pitt.edu)</u>

Chapter 21
"Our Son Anthony Takes His Own Meeting"
Anthony the Advocate

October 29, 2021: I woke up with a start at 10:30 am. I felt out of it, as if I had missed something important. That is when I realized that my alarm didn't go off this particular morning. I had overslept! For all the days for that to happen, this was not the day. My heart was racing, and I was in full panic mode. Anthony had toured the Manorville Day Hab on October 22nd and his admissions meeting was this morning.

I grabbed my cell phone immediately; it read: Reminder: 9:00 am Conference Call for Anthony's Team Meeting for Day Hab Without Walls Admissions/and Job Discussions. (Day Habilitation Without Walls is an innovative OPWDD program that suitably serves individuals by moving them from within typical Day Habilitation programs ("Within Walls") and giving them more opportunities to utilize their skills in the community ("Without Walls.")[i] This meeting was coordinated with 11 staff members, some of whom were from different agencies. Anthony had been complaining to his House Manager and his Care Manager at Advanced Care Alliance about wanting to attend day hab and work since both programs had been delayed due to the Coronavirus. I was pleased to see that they were very empathetic and compassionate towards him. I was so proud of him for expressing that he was his happiest when keeping busy - whether he was at day hab with friends and peers, performing community service, or working and earning money. He wanted independence and more for himself. What parent wouldn't be proud? Now I missed his meeting. What a terrible impression I had made…Grrr!

I called the Director of Admissions and immediately apologized for not being on the conference call. My distress was obvious. She told me that at the beginning of the call, they had waited a few minutes for me. She asked Anthony if they should wait a little longer. He replied, "No, because my mom is sad that her dad passed away and I'm sure she's home resting. I got this!" She told me that I should be very proud of him. He had taken care of business on his own. He knew exactly what he wanted, and he had advocated for himself. This was the young man that had struggled to express his emotions, had not been very verbal in his younger years, had displayed violent behaviors, and had a 90% processing delay due to seizures. As his mother, I was overcome with emotions. All I kept thinking was that the apple doesn't fall too far from the tree. Children learn behaviors and mimic their parents in good ways or bad. This was an incredible milestone for him (and for me).

Shortly afterwards, I received a phone call from Anthony:

"Hello Mom. You missed my meeting today and you've never done that before. Are you ok? I'm worried about you. I told them how sad you were because of Grandpa. Mom, I miss him very much too. I took the meeting all by myself!" I had to put the phone on mute because I had started to cry, and I didn't want him to hear me. These were happy tears though. With everything going on, I didn't want him to misinterpret my tears or emotions. When I finally unmuted the call, I had more control over myself. I explained how very proud I was of him and that he should feel a sense of pride as well.

I thought to myself that it had been a few weeks since my dad passed, and now suddenly there was a new opening at the day hab. It could very well be a coincidence, but I specifically recall asking my dad to guide and work his magic for Anthony any way he could. I would like to believe that one of his guardian angels (his grandpa) opened up that spot for him. It brought me such inner peace. My dad was always there for him in this lifetime, and that will never change for Anthony.

In the next few weeks following the meeting, Anthony would attend day hab, participate in community service, and work on a farm. When he comes home, he loves sharing his experiences with us…including how he enjoys delivering meals to the homebound elderly ("Meals on Wheels.") He now goes shopping in the community - and spends and budgets his money! He has fun going to Target, Dunkin' Donuts and Greek Bites, with a friend or in a group setting. One of his favorite things to do is working on the farm. He rakes the leaves, pulls weeds, gardens in the greenhouse, and enjoys visiting the animals. My dad's favorite pastime was gardening. Anthony explained how he felt much closer to him while he's working on the farm.

One day he went to pet one of the horses, and he thought he was going to take his hand off. He said he was surprised and scared. I asked, "Well did you bring the horse food? He probably expected some and that is why the horse reacted to you in that way." He said he's not allowed to feed the animals yet, but he's looking forward to the time when he can. The pigs are muddy, filthy and stinky. He asked, "Why do you think they like to stay in the mud like that?" I responded, "When the mud dries, it protects their skin from the harmful rays of the sun and stops bugs from biting them." He said the chickens make lots of noise and lay lots of eggs. When he leaves the farm and arrives at his group home, he is exhausted. Anthony is on his way towards becoming a true farmer!

Looking back on the day of the admissions meeting, I realized it was not meant for me to be on that conference call. My alarm didn't go off because he needed to step into his own power and use his voice. For years I had been preparing him for this moment. As he declared, "Mom, I took care of business!"

[i] http://www.ghoinc.org./programs

Chapter 22
"My Heart is Healed 100%/Alleluia"
Visit with My Cardiologist

November 16, 2021: I'm sitting in bed staring at the ceiling - not wanting to get out of bed. I have a busy morning ahead. I woke up thinking of my dad. Every day is a struggle trying to live without him in my life. Despite my best efforts, I cannot shake off this loss. I believe I never will.

I had a 9:30 am Zoom appointment with my spiritual healer, teacher and friend, Terry Lauria. I sorely needed this session with her due to the emotional whirlwind constantly blowing around and through me. Let me tell you, it's very difficult working to improve yourself, especially when some of those around you don't evolve at all or see no need for improvement in their lives. Some really don't know or care about how to help themselves. If you work on yourself, your relationship with yourself improves, and thus, the relationships you have with others improve. What you see in yourself is what you see in others. Once you know yourself well enough you can claim your own emotional baggage as your own and not someone else's. "Psychological projection" is the process of misinterpreting what is "inside" as coming from "outside". It forms the basis of empathy by the projection of personal experiences to understand someone else's subjective world.[i] It also helps in learning to meet people where they are at and not where you are at. People can only meet you at their own level of understanding themselves.

This morning Terry was giving me much needed guidance to be gentle with myself because of the deep sadness and grief, which I knew would escalate during the upcoming holidays. She has experienced so much death herself that she knows exactly what I am feeling at this point in the process. These deep conversations always ended with tears running down my face, followed by her words of encouragement. I needed to have patience with myself and others, but that seemed to be an impossible task. I didn't like being angry or short with people. That isn't who I am, and I don't like it at all. She assured me that this was normal grieving. I felt a little better after we spoke. At the end of my session with her, she had mentioned that I would soon be hearing some positive uplifting news. As always, Terry held out that shining light of optimism to help me find my way.

Soon after the meeting, I had an 11:15 am appointment for a mammogram. I'm pretty sure a man invented mammography because it is so uncomfortable and painful. Of course, my curiosity got the better of me, so I googled it. Robert Egan, MD from the University of Texas, created the device. You place your breast in between two plates, which then squeeze it tightly, while an x-ray looking for any abnormalities is taken. Now being a big- breasted woman, I have to say with no exaggeration that I leave the medical office feeling awfully sore. My other issue is that a more extensive exam is always required due to my implanted defibrillator. Does it save lives? Yes. Should you have your breasts checked? Yes. God created women because men couldn't handle what we can. Can you imagine if men had to stick their junk in there?

With my aching breasts I headed to my cardiologist's office, which is only a few blocks away, for a routine checkup. As usual, I waited at least a half an hour before seeing him. You sit, you wait, you anticipate, and you hope for the best. I usually say a few prayers under my breath while seated in the waiting room. Forty-five minutes later, the nurse and I walk down the hallway, wearing our masks, to an open room. She closes the door, asks how I'm feeling, performs the usual medications review, and takes my vitals. My blood pressure is slightly elevated. I laughed and told her, "That usually happens when I am waiting to see the doctor." I told her, "It should come down in a few minutes."

My cardiologist enters, asks the same routine questions, and then asks if I have time for a heart transmission reading. Every month, there is a technician that reads a transmission from my ICD (Implantable Cardioverter Defibrillator), which also includes a pulse generator and one or more leads that are surgically implanted into your body. The pulse generator, which constantly watches your heartbeat, is like a small computer. I have a remote monitoring pacemaker which is equipped with a special transmitter. It automatically sends medical and technical information from my heart to the cardiologist's office. I have a device on my nightstand called Merlin@home. This replaces in-clinic visits and is connected through Wi-Fi and internet. Amazing right?! Now he wanted an in-clinic reading. He was concerned about the stress I've been under since my dad's passing.

The technician comes in with the ICD reading machine and places a magnetic ring on my pacemaker. I closed my eyes for a few minutes. When I opened them, the reading on the screen came back 100%. My heart was working on its own! I wasn't sure if I had read it correctly. My cardiologist assured me that the reading was accurate… my Takotsubo Syndrome and my Ventricular Tachycardia were gone. Was this the good news that Terry was telling me about? This time, tears of gratitude and relief spilled onto my cheeks.

All of my self-love mantras, healings, meditation and calming breathing exercises had finally paid off. I'm a full-figured woman. I try to eat in moderation. I walk and don't exercise vigorously. I surround myself with positive, loving people and stay away from negative energy-sucking vampire phonies. What I always focus on is the fact that my body had been severely damaged once – *and it could easily happen again*. So, I've taught myself to control my emotions and then detach from them. Feel it and let it go. Letting go is easier said than done, but once you learn how, there is a sense of freedom. Inner peace begins the moment you choose not to allow another person or event to control your emotions.

"You will continue to suffer if you have an emotional reaction to everything that is said to you. True power is sitting back and observing everything with logic. If words control you, that means everyone else can control you. Breathe and allow things to pass."[ii]

UPDATE

Even though my heart has healed and can be regulated with medications, insurance does not approve of having the defibrillator removed because it is not a medical necessity.

[i]**www.fusingneutrons.com**
[ii] Attributed to Bruce Lee

Chapter 23
"Jake"
My Fur Baby is Getting Old

How time flies and waits for no one! Jake, our fur baby, has been with us since the Spring of 2007, and turned 15 years old on January 27th of 2023. His eyes are blinded by cataracts, and so his needs have dramatically changed. We make sure he doesn't climb the stairs, jump on or off the bed or couches, and we always pick him up for a cuddle – that's the easy part! I look into his eyes even though I know he can't see me, and I whisper, "It's Mom. I will love you forever and always keep you safe." To make him feel extra secure, I follow my words with a kiss on his snout.

Oftentimes when he searches for me in the house, he can't find me, and he starts to cry and howl. His anguish is so heartbreaking…We also need to constantly watch our feet because he has no idea of his own whereabouts. I'm sure he suffers from anxiety along with severe aches and pains, so at night I give him a chewable hemp seed. Jake enjoys spending time at the doggie day spa getting bathed and massaged in the jacuzzi for 20 minutes. I decided upon this special pampering because I know from first-hand experience how much a spa day soothes away my stress - so why not do the same for my sweet Jake?

Looking for more solutions, I purchased a Blind Dog Harness Device, but he wasn't having any part of it. If anything, he became more irritable. Hoping he would eventually acclimate to it, I would place the device on him, but he looked so miserable that I put it aside. I've been told by friends and professionals that dogs have a highly developed sense of smell, which allows them to use smell and their other senses to compensate for their lack of vision. If the loss of sight is gradual, behavior changes may be subtle and not noticeable until the dog is completely blind.

Everyone around me is getting older and needs more comfort and support. First it was my mother-in-law, my dad, my mom, and now Jake. Being highly empathetic as well as a caregiver, my heart hurts when I think too much about their decline. I've learned not to have these thoughts remain in my head for too long. I try to reset my memories and thoughts to happier times.

My Jake has been with us through the good and bad: the ups, downs, laughter and tears…birthdays celebrated together…Anthony Jr. moving into his first and last residences…dad's passing…mom moving into a nursing home, etc. He is an intrinsic link to our family history, and I do not know how we will cope without him. He has consoled all of us on so many occasions. People who say, "it's only a dog," may have never experienced the joy of having one.

Jake has helped relieve my unsurmountable amounts of stress. In fact, I am positive that he played an integral role in the healing of my physical and emotional heart issues. Overall, he brings my family sheer happiness on a daily basis. A Japanese study done in 2009 showed that just staring into a dog's eyes raises your oxytocin. Oxytocin is a hormone that's produced in the hypothalamus and released into the bloodstream by the pituitary gland. Its main function is to facilitate childbirth, which is one of the reasons it is called the "love drug" or "love hormone."[i]

Dogs stimulate our interest in people. Since both my sons are on the spectrum and found socialization so very difficult in the early years, it made perfect sense to have a dog. I believe that dogs also have an innate sense of knowing if a person is good or bad. Your dog may not know the moral decisions a person has made, but he/she can recognize signs of nervousness, anger, fear and danger. Most importantly for me now is that Jake keeps me active, even on those days when I'm sad and finding it difficult to get out of bed. To be completely honest, I have found that Jake is better than any antidepressant or anxiety drug I have ever taken in my past. I guess Jake is our emotional support dog in the way he has protected us and our home for all of these years. Life is so much better with a dog.

"Such short little lives our pets have to spend with us, and they spend most of it waiting for us to come home each day."[ii]

<u>UPDATE</u>

It is with deep sadness that Jake passed away surrounded by our loving family on November 3, 2023 and has crossed over The Rainbow Bridge. Our lives will never be the same. He will be so very missed.

[i]Healtth.Harvard.edu
[ii] John Grogan. Marley and Me: Life and Love with the World's Worst Dog

Chapter 24
"My Beautiful Mom" Emotional Move into the Nursing Home"

Dementia had my beautiful mom firmly in its grasp since my dad's passing. Primarily, she has a tremendous amount of emotional, mental and cognitive difficulties being at the home she had shared with my dad for decades. Although her live-in aide Pauline was a Godsend, my mom needed so much more. I could see that the isolation, broken up by our visits, was weakening her. She was afraid to use her walker because the hallways were very narrow, and even more worrisome was her increasing loss of basic communication skills, which led to violent reactions to any change. The lack of physical exercise was causing muscle atrophy (the wasting or thinning of muscle mass.[i] She would often wait seated at the kitchen table, near the back door, for my dad to come in from his garden. It was breaking my heart to watch her. She would forget that he passed away. I now feel that a part of her did realize he was gone because she slept in a spare room across the hall from the master bedroom that she had shared with my dad. More revealing for me was that the master bedroom was the room in which he had passed away, and she always kept that door closed.

Caregivers constantly feel that they have to give the best possible care to ensure their loved one's well-being. Sadly, it's the family who witnesses the patient slowly fading away, which has prompted many to use the sobriquet of "The Long Goodbye" for this disease called Dementia or Alzheimer's. The name makes total sense to me. I know it's easier to stay away and not witness any of this, but she is my mother, and I want to appreciate and love her while she is still here.

We received a wedding invitation for my cousin's long weekend wedding during the week of June 5, 2022 on Block Island. It was unfortunate timing since Pauline, the live-in aid, was going to be in Jamaica with her family. We wanted to attend, but how could we? One of my brothers would be attending, and I was experiencing terrible anxiety knowing that the change in aide was not going to be good for her. Intuitively, I knew what to expect, but it still did not make the decision any easier.

Fast forward to the weekend of the wedding. We were heading out east to visit Anthony Jr. at his residence in the Moriches. We were to take him to lunch and discuss a few important issues with the staff. On our way there, I received a phone call from Pauline's replacement. She sounded highly upset because my mom was angry, cursing, and violent. Mom tried hitting the aide with her cane and grabbing a knife from the kitchen. This was not my mom; this was the disease. My other brother, who was not attending the wedding, left work early to check on them. We made a desperate phone call to the home care agency to determine what to do. We were told she definitely needed an assessment for a change in medications. However, until we were able to find a nurse to physically assess the situation, we had to figure out a plan to keep both her and the aide safe.

Finally acknowledging the reality of what had taken place, I recognized it was now time to have the very difficult discussion on placing mom in a nursing home. We debated the subject, in what I like to call, "the dreaded family group text message." Some of us were realistic and some clearly were not. We all agreed that it was time. I found a nurse to assess my mom at her home through the homecare agency. We needed a document called a PRI for the nursing home to review. A Patient Review Instrument (PRI) is an assessment tool developed by the New York State Department of Health to assess selected physical, medical, and cognitive characteristics of nursing home residents, as well as to document selected services that they may receive.[ii] The nurse performed the required assessment, and now, with the PRI in hand, we begin the dreaded process of moving our mother.

I got in contact with an agency called "A Place for Mom." The agent asked me questions and with my input, gave me a list of homes. My mother didn't have Medicaid, but the paperwork had been started. She had Medicare and still lived in her home. It was such an emotional experience, but I had to push aside my raw feelings, and deal with what was in front of me. Sadly, this life-changing decision was not outside of my past experiences. Just as before, all I wanted for her was to be in a safe place with good care. The routine was the same: Call the nursing homes, speak to the admissions department, and exchange questions and answers. On top of your conflicting emotions, you also had to deal with so much red tape and unknown terms. Many of these homes were a la carte and private pay only. I needed a long-term dementia care lock-down unit with nursing, and a private pay system that would eventually transfer over to Medicaid.

I would pray to my dad daily and ask him for guidance and direction to help in my decision making. My cousin Maria would randomly pop into my head. When this happens to me, I need to ask myself why? This happens to me often. Whenever a spirit communicates so strongly, it usually means you are being divinely guided. Maria had recently placed her mother into a nursing home a few months ago. Shortly after, I spoke to her sister Donna who had handled most of the paperwork and placement. Their mother was in a smaller, but quieter dementia lock-down unit. There was no availability, and I also knew that my mom liked more interaction, but maybe there was a reason for the divine guidance. So, I called the home and set up an appointment to visit shortly after our conversation.

At the end of June, I decided to visit the nursing home. I pulled up and spotted a nurse coming out of the main building and asked how she felt about working there. She had a lovely smile and proceeded to tell me she had been an attending nurse there for 15 years. I also discovered that she was taking care of my cousin's mom. I felt really positive about the interaction. A further positive sign was that Admissions had mentioned the room that was available was #333. Angel number 333 is an indication that your angels will help you in your journey of self-acceptance and finding love. The 333 number symbolizes the presence of angels who will purge your thoughts of any negativity and replace them with pure love. In astrology it also symbolizes the alliance between mind, body, spirit and the Holy Trinity…(Father, Son and the Holy Ghost).

The PRI was reviewed by the head of nursing. Admissions told me that she would be a good fit so I took a tour of the building called Sea Cliff. My son Anthony's very first placement was at St. Christopher's - Ottilie in Sea Cliff. How everything comes back to this moment! I had used my intuition to place my son in a residential/school environment because of his disabilities and now, at this climax of my mom's life, I was making the same decisions for her. I strongly believe that my direction of Anthony's emotional journey was in preparation for this moment in time. Driving on the Seaford Oyster Bay Parkway I saw a license plate that read AAM-0009. My parents' initials Angela and Armando Marinelli, 000 is a symbol of infinite possibilities and infinity. To remind us that we are part of a larger, infinite process, our guardian angels use this method. Stay connected to your intuition to find the answers you are seeking and realize that life is coming full circle. This is the truth that has guided me. According to the Bible, "0" symbolizes God as well as His divine character, hence it is a solid number. The number 9 is powerful. It represents completion, although not a final ending—more like the fulfillment of one cycle so that you can prepare to initiate the next one. It's a recognition of life's ongoing ebb and flow. As such, I knew that the license plate would have significance. If you open yourself to the divine signs around you, you will "see" them.

I toured the Sea Cliff building with the woman from Admissions. It is not easy to witness residents in all different stages and types of dementia. Impulsivity, trouble communicating, repeating memories from the past, forgetting the present, eloping, violence, screaming outbursts, etc. are all behaviors they cannot control.

On another note, the nurses and aides were friendly, compassionate and caring. The room was bright and full of sunshine from the nearby window. Before I left, I set another date for my oldest brother and his wife to tour in order to make sure they agreed it was a good placement. A week later we toured together and finally we were all in agreement. It was a good fit for her. When I got home the same day, I filled out all of the admissions paperwork and emailed it back. I also drove the original packet to the nursing home the next day. I didn't want anything to delay the move.

We already knew it wouldn't be good enough for my other brother. Our anxieties were in overdrive because he isn't the realistic type at all. He's all about aesthetics and has no idea about the amount of care my mom really needed. It's a nursing home, not a five - star hotel. We all knew nothing would be good enough for him to actually allow him to go along with this step. It was just too difficult for him to make the time, do his own research, tour the homes, have something to compare it to and make a decision for himself since his emotions would never allow him from giving his final OK. He busied himself with his business and social obligations to distance himself from what was happening to our mother. I had granted him Power-of-Attorney because at the time I made all the medical decisions for both our parents, while my immediate family still needed my involvement - and all of it was exhausting. I appreciate all he did for our parents financially, but my other brother and I would have sold my parents' house when the market was at its highest and placed my mom sooner. He made poor financial decisions, which affected us all — particularly my mother.

The moving date was Saturday, July 9th. I now had to spend time at my parents' home in Bethpage, packing things that she needed for her move. We were so fortunate that Pauline, Mom's live-in aide, was back from Jamaica for this crucial transition. On the way to the house, I stopped at the local hardware store to pick up some storage containers. Running through my mind was a mental list of what I needed to pack for her. Does this ever get any easier? I also needed to make spare keys so my siblings could enter the house when needed.

It was the Thursday before the move, and I met my sister-in-law and Pauline at the house to explain to Mom that she was moving into the nursing home. This knot in my stomach felt very familiar. The same emotions flooded over me when I had been preparing for Anthony Jr.'s move when he was seven. We collected her summer clothing, pants, socks, undergarments, toothbrush, shoes, slippers, sleepwear, and bed comforter, along with pictures of the immediate family. The rush of memories swirled in my head. I'm no longer going to be visiting their home anymore. That's the reality. That part of my life had forever ended. Whenever I was driving on the Seaford Oyster Bay Parkway, I always got off their exit 7W to spend time with them for surprise visits - breakfast, coffee, lunch or dinner. This was to be no more. The waves of sorrow and guilt were insurmountable, but I needed to keep myself together, pressing forward and asking my dad in heaven, my guardian angels, and God himself to keep me strong, grounded and levelheaded. My heavenly spirits had to continue guiding me as they had always done throughout my life.

We were finished packing. Now we were to have coffee and discuss with my beautiful Mom that she was no longer going to live in her home. AARGH! My sister-in-law, Mom, Pauline and I headed down the hallway into the kitchen. I tried to make a pot of coffee with the percolator, and for some reason, the first time it would not perk - wrong chord. The second time, too many damn seeds. The third time, Pauline took over and the coffee was perfect. We poured the coffee and we all sat at the kitchen table. I grabbed her hand, looked into her eyes and said, "I love you so much and I would do anything for you." I asked, "Do you want to live in this house anymore?" She said, "No, not really. Too many memories." I could only assume she meant my dad. I knew she was lonely. I took a very deep breath, and we continued our conversation. Still holding her hand and looking into her eyes, "Mom, we found you a nursing home." She responded "Ok." My sister-in-law asked, "Do you think she understands what you're saying?" I felt intuitively that she did. We both held back our tears, waited a little while, and hugged mom goodbye. She seemed fine. How much of it was dementia? I guess we will never know. On the way out my sister-in-law explained that my husband and I needed to move her because she had a funeral to attend. I knew what needed to be done, and that it wasn't going to be easy, but I was determined to get it done. I did not sleep that Thursday or Friday before moving her in. Between menopause, anxiety, emotions and self -doubt, how could I sleep?

It was now Saturday, and we had packed my husband's car the night before. No amount of coffee was going to sustain us. Something I just knew. When you're emotionally drained and your soul is tired, caffeine is absolutely no help. We got washed and dressed, and neither one of us could eat a thing. I took some protein bars and fruit with us. My husband hugged me before we were about to leave and said, "I love you and it's all going to be alright." We got into the car and left to pick up Mom and Pauline.

We arrived…Mom was ready and waiting by the door. She was ready to leave. I will never know how much she understood at this point. She was not returning to her home. I had a huge lump in my throat. I looked at the pink rose bush in front of my parents' home and there it was - one single rose. My Dad!! When I would leave their home, he would cut me a single rose and sing, "Piccolo Fiore, Dove Vai?" In English it means, "My little flower, where are you going?" It brought me so much peace. At that very moment, I knew he was with us - and all was going to be alright.

We arrived at the nursing home and went to the main building to drop off all of her clothing to be labeled and to pick up some paperwork. Unfortunately, it was the weekend and there was only a skeleton crew. It didn't feel or seem as if anyone was expecting us. That wasn't good, considering my mom had dementia and we needed for this move to go smoothly. After 45 minutes of confusion and frustration we were finally met by a lovely woman - Felicia from Human Resources. She made a few phone calls, took down our information and told us to meet her at the Sea Cliff Building. Time was moving so slowly on this particular day.

We arrived at the Sea Cliff building, and my husband opened the trunk and packed all of her belongings onto a cart. I waited for Pauline as she escorted Mom from the car into the building. We signed in, took our Covid Tests and followed Felicia into the elevator. We waited in the lounge area because the room needed some cleaning. Mom sat with Pauline, ate some lunch, and appeared comfortable. Felicia and the staff were also very comforting to us. We were introduced to all the staff and took care of more intake questions. A half an hour passed and then Felicia took us to her bedroom. I fixed her bed with her favorite comforter of the Virgin Mary, placed all of the pictures on her dresser, and all of the toiletries in her bathroom. I poured holy water into my hand, made the sign of the cross and placed my hand onto the door, and asked the Lord for peace and grace in this space, which I followed with the Lord's Prayer, Hail Mary, and the Glory Be. I heard my dad's voice telling me he would watch over her. We escorted her into the main dining area and the staff told us not to say good-bye. This was the same exact routine we went through with Anthony Jr. to prevent a temper tantrum or meltdown when we left him there, the memory of which still flickers deep inside of me.

I visited her that entire week. It was more of an ordeal for me than it was for her. She was content every time I would go visit. I would bring a Medium Caramel Swirl Iced Latte from Dunkin' Donuts, her favorite food and snacks. On July 28th we celebrated her 80th birthday there. The staff escorted my brother, sister-in-law, my husband, myself and son Michael to the private lounge area through the main corridor. We had flowers, strawberry shortcake, a birthday crown, fruit, and cookies. She was so happy that we were all together. We made some video calls so family members could wish her a happy birthday. We talked, laughed, and joked as in old times. She was so happy to be with all of us celebrating together. It's always a good day when she can find her words and communicate. She said it was one of the best days ever! She lived to spend time with her family.

On the way out, there was this man seated near the entrance screaming, "Hey, Hey, Hey!" I was walking up ahead with Mom, with everyone following behind, and my husband taking up the rear of this procession. My husband looked at the gentleman and asked, "Can I help you? Do you need anything?" He looked at my husband and screamed "You're an asshole!" We all looked at each other and burst into laughter. The sad part about it is the residents can't control what they say or do. They don't choose to be like this. It's just the way it is.

At the end of this chapter, I've come to the conclusion that I need to forgive my brother, not so much for him, but more for myself. It's just too heavy a burden to carry. I did my best for both of my parents, and I spent many years of quality time with them. In the end, I made the difficult decision that had to be made for her own safety and well-being. I am able to put my head on the pillow at night and sleep soundly knowing this. I worked tirelessly to heal our past and present relationship. It was a long journey of self-reflection but in the end, I forgave him.

I will leave you with this.......

"You may want to forgive your parents for: Raising you through their own unresolved trauma. Not being able to teach you certain skills, because nobody taught them. Not being able to understand you because they did not have the capacity. Raising you through their own struggles, worries, pain, and fears. Doing their best with what they knew and had. Following certain cultural norms that surrounded them. Being emotionally unavailable, just as their parents were emotionally unavailable.

In other words, love them for who they are not."[iii]

[i]Clevelandclinic.org
[ii]NYconnects.gov
[iii] The Minds Journal

I See You

I see you running your child to therapy when your friends are running their kids to Little League or ballet

I see you slipping out of the conversation when your friends are all chiming in about milestones and test grades.

I see you constantly juggling appointments and meetings.

I see you sitting at your computer for hours researching what your child needs.

I see you cringe when people whine about what feels like petty things.

I see you spread thin but still going the extra mile for your family.

I see you digging for depths of strength you never dreamed you had.

I see you showing appreciation to the teachers, therapists and medical professionals who serve your child with you.

I see you rising early in the morning to do it all again after another chaotic night.

I see you when you're hanging on to the end of your rope for dear life.

I know you feel invisible, like nobody notices any of it. But I want you to know I notice you. I see you relentlessly pushing onward.

I see you keep choosing to do everything in your power to give your child the best possible care at home, in school, at therapy and the doctor.

What you're doing matters. It's worth it.

On those days when you wonder if you can do it another minute, I want you to know I see you.

I want you to know you're beautiful.

I want you to know it's worth it.

I want you to know you aren't alone.

I want you to know love is what matters most, and you have that nailed.

And on those days when you have breakthroughs, those times when the hard work pays off and success is yours to cherish, I see you then too, and I am proud of you.

Whichever day today is, you're worthy, you're good and I see you.

~Alethea Mshar

ACKNOWLEDGEMENTS

My sons Anthony and Michael, for they have challenged and inspired me to become the mother and woman I am today.

My husband and father to our sons, Anthony, for believing in me and our family.

My parents and mom-in-law, Armando, Angela and Frances, are the backbone and foundation of our family. They have taught me the true meaning of faith and determination.

My spiritual healer Terry Lauria, who gave me solid advice, compassion, and understanding when times were difficult. Helped me evolve into who I am.

A special thanks to my editor, Linda Pedreira, a one-of-a-kind lady, without whom I could not have taken this journey.

Thanks to GOD for making all things possible, showing me that miracles do exist, confirming the true power of prayer and intuition.

My BFF Patty, for always having my back and believing in me… My soul-sister and cousin Donna, who always knows what I need, even when I don't…Soul-sister and spiritual gangster Sharon who delivers wisdom and insight on cue… Susan and Michael of "Susan's Singing Bowls," the gift that keeps on giving and healing. My life has changed for the better since meeting them on my path to healing. Kenny the amazing magical tech guy for his knowledge in graphics. Jillian for her creativity, and generous and loving big heart. Matt for being there for our sons, giving them such great advice and support. Greg and Alex for loving and accepting our sons unconditionally. Toniann Russo of Gypsy Gems who creates handmade, unique, beautiful pieces of jewelry for me. My outfits are not complete without them.

Melissa Baculy and Tracey Henderson, Residential Supervisors at I.G.H.L. and Mr. Christopher Brady, Director of Clinical Services at C.D.D. Ms. Joanne Lupo, Mr. Michael Wells, Mr. Ivan Rivera, Matthew Valentine and Kevin Flynn, former employees of C.D.D., who were amazing teachers and role models with the patience, dedication and support for our son Anthony and his peers.

Danielle Brooks, Maria Girardi Licata and Paulette Palmer of the Special Kids Advocates Agency for their friendship, advocacy, and support of my special needs children.

Coaches LaBella, Hoffman and Weiss for teaching team sportsmanship and setting a good example. Challenger Division Little League for giving Anthony the opportunity he would never have had.

Thanks to Laura Ryan Photography, not only for her patience, but her beautiful work.

For those of you I have not mentioned, I sincerely thank you for being the angels on earth that have crossed my path and who have played a special role in raising both my children.

Dedications to My Friends and Loved Ones That are No Longer With Us

Spiritual healer, and confidante in heaven: Maureen Polinice.

My beautiful Godmother, Silvana Puleo, who loved and supported me unconditionally. She always gave me peace in my heart.

Diedre Hallett, my other mother, for encouraging me to push forward and never letting me forget my inner strength.

Loretta Russo, my neighbor, who watched and supported our babies as they grew up into men.

Anthony Ievolello, my best friend's husband, and Godfather to our son Michael. He was a generous, kind, and loving man to both our children and helped them become the young men they are today. He created the brilliant idea of our son leaving the nest as Harry Potter and going to Hogwarts School of Witchcraft and Wizardry.

Tanya Brugger, dedicated teacher's assistant at C.D.D., where she also worked as an aide in the Children's Residence and became Anthony's second mom.

Nick Boba, former Managing Director of C. D. D., who lived for and loved the special needs children, and advocated valiantly for every one of them.

Thanks to the entire staff at C.D.D. and I.G.H.L. for being "the village" in raising my son Anthony. As a parent of a special needs child, I am a lifelong member of a unique club of people with a common bond, that of sharing the joys and challenges of raising children who are specially gifted.

The staff at C.D.D. and I.G.H.L. are part of my club too. You have chosen to share your amazing skills, compassion, and gifts with my child. You certainly had the choice to do other things and use your many talents elsewhere. I am glad you chose to be part of the C.D.D. and I.G.H.L. family, and I am grateful for what each of you gives of yourself every day to make our children's days brighter and more meaningful. My son is a better person for having known you. You have made a very positive difference in his life -- and in mine! Thank you for all that you do, and for being part of my club and the C.D.D./I.G.H.L. family!

Love & light,

Catherine Marinelli-Gagliano

Can You Help My Mom?

Thank You For Reading My Mom's Book!

My mom really appreciates all of your feedback, and we love hearing what you have to say.
She needs your input to make the next version of her next book and her future books even better.
Please leave her an honest review on Amazon letting her know what you thought of the book.

Thanks so much in advance.
Anthony, Jr., Michael
 & Jake